scrumptious

from THE GIRL WHO ATE EVERYTHING
CHRISTY DENNEY

SHADOW
MOUNTAIN

To the greatest taste
testers in the world—
my husband, John,
and kids, Austin, Brock,
Weston, Grace, and Bailey

Food photography by Christy Denney

Visit us at shadowmountain.com

Library of Congress Cataloging-in-Publication Data

Names: Denney, Christy, 1980– author.
Title: Scrumptious : from the girl who ate everything / Christy Denney. Description: [Salt Lake City] : Shadow Mountain, [2021] | Includes index. | Summary: "Food blogger Christy Denney, also known as 'The Girl Who Ate Everything,' shares her favorite quick-and-easy and tried-and-true recipes that are perfect for weekday family meals as well as for large groups and parties."—Provided by publisher.
Identifiers: LCCN 2021018072 | ISBN 978-1-62972-933-6 (paperback) | ISBN 978-1-62972-967-1 (hardcover)
Subjects: LCSH: Cooking, American. | BISAC: COOKING / Courses & Dishes / General | COOKING / General | LCGFT: Cookbooks.
Classification: LCC TX715 .D41 2021 | DDC 641.5973—dc23
LC record available at https://lccn.loc.gov/2021018072

Printed in China
RR Donnelley, Dongguan, China

10 9 8 7 6 5 4 3 2 1

contents

one-pan dinners

feeding a crowd

game-day eats

low-carb favorites

quick and easy

tried and true

something sweet

one-pan dinners

One-pan meals are my go-to when I need an easy fuss-free meal. Busy weeknights call for these simple meals that the whole family loves. Dishes? There's only one to do! Cleanup doesn't get any easier than this.

‹ Sheet Pan Steak and Parmesan Potatoes P. 29

BLT Pasta

Prep: 5 minutes • Cook: 20 minutes • Serves 4

There's something about the flavors in the classic BLT that just make magic. In this simple pasta dish, the "lettuce" is spinach paired with salty bacon and fresh tomatoes.

8 ounces bacon, chopped

1 cup diced yellow onion

2 cloves garlic, minced

2 cups low-sodium
  chicken broth

8 ounces short pasta

3 cups baby spinach

¾ cup shredded or grated
  Parmesan cheese

½ cup cherry tomatoes,
  quartered

1. In a large skillet, cook bacon over medium heat until browned and crispy. Drain on paper towels. Reserve 1 tablespoon bacon grease in pan and discard the rest.

2. Sauté onion in bacon grease until soft. Add garlic and cook for an additional minute.

3. Add chicken broth and pasta. Cover and bring to a boil. Reduce heat to medium-low. Cook about 10 minutes, stirring occasionally, until pasta is tender.

4. Once pasta is done, stir in spinach until it wilts. Sir in Parmesan cheese and top with tomatoes.

SCRUMPTIOUS TIP

Short pasta, as the name suggests, is any pasta that is short in length. A few popular short pastas are farfalle, fusilli, macaroni, penne, and rigatoni.

Salsa Verde Chicken Skillet

Prep: 5 minutes • Cook: 30 minutes • Serves 6

I grew up in Arizona, so Mexican food was always part of my family's get-togethers, holidays, and every-day life. Now, every time I make a Mexican dish, I feel like I'm home.

2 tablespoons vegetable oil

1 pound boneless skinless chicken breasts, cut into 1-inch pieces

1 teaspoon kosher salt

2 cloves garlic, minced

2 cups salsa verde

1 cup low-sodium chicken broth

1 cup long-grain white rice

15 ounces black beans, rinsed and drained

2 cups shredded Mexican-style cheese, divided

TOPPINGS

diced avocado

sour cream

pico de gallo

1. In a large skillet, heat oil over medium heat. Add chicken and sprinkle with salt. Cook until chicken is browned, about 3 minutes on each side. Set chicken aside.

2. Add garlic to skillet and cook for 30 seconds. Stir in salsa verde, chicken broth, and rice. Bring mixture to a boil. Cover and reduce heat to a simmer. Cook for 15 to 20 minutes, stirring occasionally, until rice is done and liquid has been absorbed.

3. Stir in the cooked chicken, black beans, and 1 cup Mexican cheese. Sprinkle remaining cup cheese on top. Cover and let cheese melt.

4. Top with desired toppings and serve immediately.

SCRUMPTIOUS TIP

Salsa verde means "green sauce" and is popular in Mexican cuisine. Traditionally it's a sauce made of tomatillos, finely chopped onion, garlic, cilantro, parsley, and hot peppers. This sauce is packed with so much flavor that it's a great addition to any recipe.

One-Pan Spinach Lasagna

Prep: 5 minutes • Cook: 30 minutes • Serves 8

One of the first meals I ever made for my husband when we were dating was lasagna. I remember thinking, "Wow, this is a lot of work!" Turns out, it doesn't have to be. This one-pan version is quick and easy with all of the classic flavors of lasagna.

1 pound mild Italian sausage

4 cloves garlic, minced

8 ounces lasagna noodles, broken into 2-inch-long pieces, or farfalle pasta

4 cups (32 ounces) marinara sauce

2 cups spinach

4 ounces fresh mozzarella, sliced

½ cup whole-milk ricotta cheese

¼ cup grated Parmesan cheese

torn fresh basil leaves for topping

1. In a large skillet, cook sausage over medium-high heat until browned. Add garlic and cook for an additional 30 seconds.

2. Add lasagna noodles and pour marinara sauce on top. Bring mixture to a boil. Cover and reduce heat to a simmer. Cook for 15 to 20 minutes or until noodles are tender.

3. Stir in spinach and top with mozzarella and ricotta. Cover to let cheese melt. Sprinkle with Parmesan cheese and garnish with basil.

SCRUMPTIOUS TIP

I love the texture and flavor of fresh mozzarella but don't always have it on hand. You can substitute shredded mozzarella in this recipe.

Easy Beef Stir-Fry

Prep: 5 minutes • Cook: 15 minutes • Serves 4

This meal is a great way to eat veggies. You can add whatever veggies you have on hand.

2 tablespoons vegetable oil

1 pound beef sirloin or flank steak, cut into 2-inch strips

1½ cups broccoli florets

1 red bell pepper, cut into strips

1 cup matchstick carrots

¼ cup sliced green onion

2 cloves garlic, minced

2 tablespoons low-sodium soy sauce

1 tablespoon brown sugar

1 tablespoon sesame oil

1 teaspoon sriracha

2 tablespoons toasted sesame seeds

1. In a large skillet or wok, heat oil over medium-high heat. Add beef and cook until browned, about 4 minutes.

2. Move beef to side of pan. Add broccoli, red bell pepper, carrots, and green onion. Cook vegetables for about 3 minutes. Add garlic and cook for an additional 30 seconds.

3. Stir in soy sauce and brown sugar. Cook until vegetables reach desired tenderness.

4. Drizzle with sesame oil and sriracha. Sprinkle with toasted sesame seeds.

One-Pan Chicken Enchilada Skillet

Prep: 5 minutes • Cook: 10 minutes • Serves 6

This easy chicken enchilada skillet can be ready in ten minutes. Simmer some rotisserie chicken in enchilada sauce and salsa, then stir in sliced tortillas and cook until they become nice and soft. Top this one-pan meal with cheese and all of your favorite toppings, like guacamole, sour cream, and green onion.

2 cups shredded rotisserie chicken

½ teaspoon ground cumin

½ teaspoon dried oregano

1 (10-ounce) can red enchilada sauce

½ cup chunky salsa

¼ cup water

4 (6-inch) flour tortillas, cut into 1-inch strips

1 cup shredded Mexican-style cheese

TOPPINGS

guacamole

½ cup sour cream

¼ cup sliced green onion

1. Place rotisserie chicken in a large skillet. Sprinkle with cumin and oregano. Add enchilada sauce, salsa, and water. Bring mixture to a simmer over medium heat for a couple of minutes to let the sauce thicken and the chicken heat through.

2. Stir in tortilla strips until tortillas start to soften. Sprinkle with cheese. Remove from heat and let cheese melt.

3. Top with guacamole and sour cream as desired and sprinkle with green onion. Serve immediately.

SCRUMPTIOUS TIP

An easy way to cut the tortillas into nice even strips is to stack 2 to 3 tortillas on top of each other and slice with a pizza cutter.

Alfredo Gnocchi and Broccoli Bake

Prep: 5 minutes • Cook: 20 minutes • Serves 4

The one vegetable that none of my kids complain about is broccoli. They love it! Especially covered in alfredo sauce with soft gnocchi dumplings.

3 cups low-sodium chicken broth

3 cups broccoli florets

16 ounces gnocchi

4 ounces cream cheese, softened

1 tablespoon lemon juice

1 teaspoon garlic powder

1 teaspoon kosher salt

½ teaspoon crushed red pepper flakes

2 cups shredded mozzarella cheese, divided

grated Parmesan cheese for topping

1. Preheat oven to 400 degrees F.

2. In a large oven-safe saucepan, bring chicken broth to a boil. Add broccoli and gnocchi. Cover. Cook over medium heat for 5 to 7 minutes or until broccoli is tender and gnocchi floats to the top.

3. Stir in cream cheese, lemon juice, garlic powder, salt, and crushed red pepper flakes until cream cheese dissolves.

4. Stir in 1 cup mozzarella cheese. Sprinkle remaining cup mozzarella cheese on top. Bake for 4 to 6 minutes or until cheese is bubbly.

5. Sprinkle with Parmesan cheese and serve.

SCRUMPTIOUS TIP

What is gnocchi? Gnocchi is a type of pasta made of flour, eggs, and mashed potatoes, though many people consider it to be a dumpling. It's known for its rolled shape. Gnocchi can be found in the pasta aisle in the grocery store.

Sheet Pan Pork Tenderloin

Prep: 5 minutes • Cook: 30 minutes • Serves 6

Tender pork with sweet potatoes and green beans is a complete dinner all in one pan. I love how the savory pork marinated in a Dijon mustard sauce pairs so well with the sweetness of the potatoes.

1 ¼ pounds pork tenderloin, sliced

3 tablespoons olive oil, divided

1 tablespoon Dijon mustard

1 tablespoon maple syrup

3 cloves garlic, minced

½ teaspoon dried oregano

salt and freshly ground black pepper

10 ounces butternut squash or sweet potato, cubed

8 ounces trimmed green beans, cut into 1-inch pieces

1. Preheat oven to 400 degrees F. Line a large baking sheet with aluminum foil or spray with nonstick cooking spray.

2. Place pork slices on the pan and drizzle 1 tablespoon olive oil, mustard, maple syrup, garlic, oregano, salt, and pepper. Arrange slices on one side of the baking sheet in an even layer.

3. Place butternut squash or sweet potato on the other side of the baking sheet and drizzle with 1 tablespoon olive oil, salt, and pepper. Arrange squash or potatoes on the other side of the baking sheet.

4. Bake for 20 minutes, then check temperature of pork. If done, remove and keep warm. If not, the pork will continue to cook with the green beans in the next step.

5. Flip butternut squash (and pork, if not done). Add green beans to the pan and drizzle with remaining tablespoon olive oil, salt, and pepper. Bake for 5 to 7 minutes or until green beans are done and pork has reached at least 145 degrees F. Serve.

SCRUMPTIOUS TIP

People often associate pork with dry, chewy meat because so often it's overcooked, but pork cooked correctly is tender and delicious. The best thing you can do for your meat is invest in a meat thermometer and ensure meat reaches proper cooking temperatures. Pork is done when it reaches 145 degrees F.

Cajun Sausage and Rice Skillet

Prep: 5 minutes · Cook: 30 minutes · Serves 4

In this recipe, spicy andouille sausage is cooked with bell peppers, onion, and garlic in a vibrant tomato sauce. This quick and easy dinner is packed with flavor!

1 tablespoon olive oil

14 ounces andouille sausage, cut into ¼-inch-thick slices

1 green bell pepper, sliced into strips

½ cup diced yellow onion

4 cloves garlic, minced

2 ¼ cups low-sodium chicken broth

5 tablespoons tomato paste

1 cup long-grain white rice

1 teaspoon paprika

½ teaspoon oregano

½ teaspoon kosher salt

ground black pepper to taste

chopped parsley for garnish

1. In a large skillet, heat olive oil over medium-high heat. Add sausage and cook until browned on both sides.

2. Add green bell pepper and yellow onion. Sauté for 2 to 3 minutes or until veggies are soft. Add garlic and cook for an additional minute.

3. Stir in chicken broth, tomato paste, rice, paprika, oregano, salt, and pepper. Cover and bring mixture to a boil. Reduce heat to medium-low. Simmer for 15 to 20 minutes, stirring occasionally, until rice is tender and liquid has been absorbed. Garnish with chopped parsley.

SCRUMPTIOUS TIP

Andouille sausage and kielbasa are often confused with each other because they look similar. Kielbasa is any type of meat sausage made in Poland, whereas andouille is a Cajun pork sausage that is more heavily smoked and spiced.

One-Pan Creamy Spinach Artichoke Pasta

Prep: 5 minutes • Cook: 30 minutes • Serves 6

Think of your favorite spinach artichoke dip but in pasta form. You can have this easy one-pan dinner on your table in less than twenty minutes.

1 tablespoon unsalted butter

2 cloves garlic, minced

¼ teaspoon crushed red pepper flakes

4 cups low-sodium chicken broth

2 cups heavy cream

1 pound penne pasta or any short pasta

1 teaspoon kosher salt

¼ teaspoon ground black pepper

4 ounces cream cheese, softened

1 cup grated Parmesan cheese

4 cups spinach, chopped

1 (6-ounce) jar marinated artichokes, drained and chopped

1. In a large deep skillet, melt butter over medium heat. Add garlic and red pepper flakes. Sauté for 30 seconds.

2. Add chicken broth, cream, pasta, salt, and pepper. Bring to a boil. Cover and reduce heat to medium-low. Simmer for 15 to 20 minutes, stirring occasionally, until pasta is tender.

3. Stir in cream cheese and Parmesan until melted and combined.

4. Add spinach and artichokes. Cook for 3 to 4 minutes or until spinach wilts. (The longer the sauce simmers, the thicker it becomes. It will also thicken when taken off the heat.) Serve and enjoy.

SCRUMPTIOUS TIP

This pasta meal is so versatile. Here are some things you can add or substitute to change things up.

- Use kale or arugula instead of spinach.
- Use 1 teaspoon garlic powder instead of minced garlic.
- Add some sun-dried tomatoes or a can of drained diced tomatoes.
- Add sautéed mushrooms.
- Add sautéed onions.
- Add broccoli, asparagus, or zucchini.
- Add some fresh basil.

Chicken Fried Rice

Prep: 5 minutes • Cook: 25 minutes • Serves 6

Chicken fried rice can be intimidating, but it's actually so easy, and it's all made in one pan! This is a great way to use up leftover rice.

1 tablespoon vegetable oil

1 pound boneless skinless chicken breasts, diced

salt and pepper to taste

3 tablespoons unsalted butter, divided

3 large eggs, lightly beaten

4 cups long-grain white rice, cooked and cooled

2 tablespoons low-sodium soy sauce, plus more to taste

1 tablespoon sesame oil, plus more to taste

1 cup frozen peas and carrots

¼ cup sliced green onion

1. In a large skillet, heat vegetable oil over medium-high heat. Season chicken with salt and pepper. Cook chicken for 4 to 5 minutes on each side or until browned and cooked through. Transfer to a plate and set aside. Wipe out pan if needed.

2. Reduce heat to medium. Add 1 tablespoon butter to pan and cook eggs until scrambled. Transfer to plate with chicken. Wipe out pan if needed.

3. Melt remaining 2 tablespoons butter in pan. Add rice in an even layer. Let rice sit, without stirring, over medium-high heat for 1 to 2 minutes so it gets nice and crispy.

4. Stir in soy sauce and sesame oil, coating the rice. Add frozen peas and carrots and stir until thawed. Stir in green onion.

5. Add chicken and eggs back to pan, stirring well. Add more soy sauce and sesame oil to taste. Season with salt and pepper to taste. Serve immediately.

SCRUMPTIOUS TIP

Cooked and cooled rice is the best for this recipe, otherwise your rice can turn out gummy. This recipe is ideal for leftover rice that has been stored in the refrigerator.

Cheesy Taco Pasta Shells

Prep: 5 minutes • Cook: 20 minutes • Serves 10

I keep pantry items like tomato sauce and green chiles on hand so I can make a quick meal like this at a moment's notice. Ground beef and a salsa tomato sauce with all of the seasonings make this pasta craveable.

1 pound ground beef

½ cup diced yellow onion

4 cloves garlic, minced

2 tablespoons flour

2 cups low-sodium beef broth

1 cup salsa

1 (15-ounce) can tomato sauce

1 (4-ounce) can diced green chiles

8 ounces medium pasta shells

1 ½ teaspoons chili powder

1 teaspoon dried oregano

½ teaspoon ground cumin

¾ cup heavy cream

2 cups shredded cheddar cheese

½ cup chopped cilantro

1. In a large saucepan, brown beef until no longer pink. Drain. Add onion and cook until onion is soft. Add garlic and cook for an additional minute. Sprinkle with flour and cook for an additional minute.

2. Whisk in beef broth. Add salsa, tomato sauce, green chiles, pasta shells, chili powder, oregano, and cumin. Bring to a boil. Reduce heat to a simmer, cover, and cook for 6 to 8 minutes, stirring occasionally, until pasta shells are done.

3. Stir in cream and cheddar cheese. Sprinkle with cilantro and top with your favorite taco toppings, such as sour cream and guacamole. Serve.

Garlic Honey Shrimp and Broccoli

Prep: 20 minutes • Cook: 15 minutes • Serves 4

The flavors in this meal are out of this world. The honey and soy sauce make a sweet and savory glaze that the shrimp are cooked in. You can serve this over rice or keep it low-carb and eat it by itself.

½ cup honey

¼ cup low-sodium soy sauce

1 tablespoon minced garlic

1 teaspoon grated fresh ginger

¼ teaspoon red pepper flakes

1 pound large shrimp, peeled and deveined

1 tablespoon olive oil

2 cups broccoli florets

salt and pepper to taste

2 tablespoons unsalted butter

sliced green onion for garnish

1. In a small bowl, stir together honey, soy sauce, garlic, ginger, and red pepper flakes.

2. Place shrimp in a bowl and pour half of the marinade on top. Reserve the other half for later. Toss shrimp in marinade, coating well. Let sit for 15 minutes.

3. While shrimp marinates, cook broccoli. In a large skillet, heat olive oil over medium-high heat. Add broccoli and season with salt and pepper. Sauté until broccoli is soft, about 5 minutes. Remove from pan and set aside.

4. In the skillet, melt butter over medium-high heat. Add marinated shrimp, discarding used marinade. Cook until shrimp turns pink, about 2 minutes on each side.

5. Add reserved marinade and bring to a simmer. Add broccoli and toss until well coated. Season with more salt and pepper as needed.

6. Garnish with green onion and serve immediately.

SCRUMPTIOUS TIP

I don't use a lot of fresh ginger, so I cut leftover ginger into big pieces and freeze it. Then I can thaw a piece and grate it into soups or dressings as needed.

One-Pan Chicken Fajita Rice

Prep: 5 minutes • Cook: 30 minutes • Serves 6

This chicken fajita rice is an easy one-pan Mexican dinner ready in under thirty minutes. Chicken, rice, cheese, peppers, guacamole, and sour cream make this chicken recipe a winner!

3 tablespoons unsalted butter, divided

½ cup diced white onion

½ cup diced red bell pepper

½ cup diced green bell pepper

1 clove garlic, minced

1 cup long-grain white rice

2 ¾ cups low-sodium chicken broth

¼ cup sour cream

2 cups shredded rotisserie chicken

1 (4.5-ounce) can diced green chiles

1 lime, juiced (about 1 tablespoon juice)

1 teaspoon salt

½ teaspoon ground cumin

½ teaspoon chili powder

1 cup shredded cheddar cheese

TOPPINGS

sour cream

guacamole

diced tomatoes

cilantro

1. In a large skillet, melt 2 tablespoons butter. Add onion and bell peppers. Cook for about 3 minutes or until veggies soften. Add garlic and cook for an additional minute.

2. Push vegetables to one side of the pan and melt remaining tablespoon butter. Add rice and toast for 1 to 2 minutes.

3. Add chicken broth, sour cream, rotisserie chicken, diced chiles, lime juice, salt, cumin, and chili powder. Bring mixture to a boil. Reduce heat to a simmer and cover. Cook for about 15 to 20 minutes or until rice is tender. You can add more broth and continue cooking as needed until rice finishes.

4. Sprinkle with cheese and cover until cheese melts.

5. Garnish with sour cream, guacamole, diced tomatoes, and cilantro. Serve immediately.

Sheet Pan Steak and Parmesan Potatoes

Prep: 5 minutes • Cook: 25 minutes • Serves 4

This steak dinner is gourmet without all of the hard work. The Parmesan-crusted potatoes are worthy enough to be fought over on their own. Any cut of steak can be used, but sirloin is the best bang for your buck.

1 ½ pounds red potatoes, quartered

4 tablespoons olive oil, divided

5 tablespoons grated Parmesan, divided

4 cloves garlic, minced, divided

salt and pepper to taste

1 ½ pounds sirloin steak, cut into 1-inch pieces

1 pound asparagus, ends trimmed

1. Preheat oven to 450 degrees F. Spray a large sheet pan with nonstick cooking spray.

2. Place potatoes on sheet pan. Drizzle with 2 tablespoons olive oil, 2 tablespoons Parmesan, 1 clove garlic, and salt and pepper to taste. Toss together well and spread evenly on pan. Bake for 6 to 8 minutes or until potatoes start to brown.

3. While potatoes cook, prepare steak. In a medium bowl, combine steak, 1 tablespoon olive oil, 2 tablespoons Parmesan, 2 cloves garlic, and salt and pepper to taste.

4. When potatoes are done partially cooking, push potatoes to the side of the pan and add steak in an even layer.

5. Lay asparagus next to steak. Drizzle with remaining tablespoon olive oil and sprinkle with remaining tablespoon Parmesan cheese and remaining garlic clove. Add salt and pepper to taste.

6. Bake for 6 to 8 minutes or until all ingredients reach desired doneness. Serve with additional grated Parmesan.

One-Pan Sweet Potato Black Bean Skillet

Prep: 10 minutes • Cook: 35 minutes • Serves 8

In my house, my family believes a meal without meat doesn't count as dinner. This vegetarian dish, however, is hearty enough that no one misses the meat! But feel free to add some protein, such as ground turkey or beef.

2 cups peeled and cubed sweet potatoes

1 cup water

2 tablespoons olive oil

¼ cup diced red onion

½ cup diced red bell pepper

2 cloves garlic, minced

1 cup long-grain white rice

2 cups low-sodium chicken broth

1 (15-ounce) can diced tomatoes, undrained

1 cup frozen corn

1 teaspoon chili powder

1 teaspoon cumin

3 tablespoons lime juice

salt and pepper to taste

1½ cups shredded cheddar cheese, divided

TOPPINGS

sour cream

guacamole

tomatoes

cilantro

1. In a large skillet, bring sweet potatoes and water to a boil over medium-high heat. Cover and cook for 5 to 7 minutes or until sweet potatoes are slightly tender. Add more water as needed.

2. Push potatoes to the side of the pan. Add olive oil, red onion, and red bell pepper. Cook for 2 to 3 minutes or until soft. Add garlic and cook for an additional minute.

3. Add rice and stir until coated. Stir in chicken broth, diced tomatoes, corn, chili powder, and cumin. Bring mixture to a boil, then reduce heat to a simmer. Cover and cook for 15 to 20 minutes or until rice is cooked and tender.

4. Stir in lime juice. Add salt and pepper to taste. Stir in 1 cup cheese. Sprinkle remaining ½ cup cheese on top. Replace lid and let cheese melt.

5. Serve immediately with desired toppings, like sour cream, guacamole, tomatoes, and cilantro.

Chicken Orzo

Prep: 5 minutes • Cook: 25 minutes • Serves 8

Carrots, celery, and onion are the base for any good comfort meal. Using rotisserie chicken puts this meal on the table in under thirty minutes!

1 tablespoon olive oil

1 tablespoon unsalted butter

1 cup diced carrots

1 cup diced celery

1 cup diced white onion

4 cloves garlic, minced

6 cups low-sodium chicken broth

¼ cup fresh lemon juice

1 pound orzo pasta

1 teaspoon kosher salt

¼ teaspoon ground black pepper

2 cups shredded rotisserie chicken

¾ cup grated Parmesan cheese

¼ cup chopped parsley

1. In a large skillet, heat oil and butter over medium-high heat. Sauté carrots, celery, and onion until soft. Add garlic and cook for an additional minute.

2. Stir in chicken broth, lemon juice, orzo, salt, and pepper. Bring mixture to a boil then reduce to a simmer. Cover and cook for 20 minutes or until orzo is cooked and liquid is absorbed.

3. Stir in rotisserie chicken until heated through. Stir in Parmesan cheese and parsley. Serve warm.

feeding
a crowd

If there's one thing I know, it's how to make
food for a lot of people. I'm the youngest of
ten kids, so there was always a full house of
hungry people. Whether it's breakfast or dinner,
I've got you covered on feeding the troops.

‹ Twice-Baked Potato Casserole P. 55

Panzanella Salad

Prep: 10 minutes • Cook: 15 minutes • Serves 10

Whenever I order a salad from a restaurant, my husband teases me because I eat absolutely everything in the salad except the lettuce. This panzanella salad is my kind of salad. It's got all of the good stuff and none of the lettuce.

1 (14-ounce) loaf French bread, cubed (about 6 cups)

2 tablespoons olive oil

2 tablespoons unsalted butter, melted

1 teaspoon kosher salt

1 cup cherry tomatoes, halved

1 cucumber, seeded and cubed

2 cups sliced bell pepper (any color)

½ cup sliced red onion

¼ cup basil leaves, chopped

DRESSING

½ cup olive oil

¼ cup red wine vinegar

2 cloves garlic, minced

½ teaspoon Dijon mustard

½ teaspoon kosher salt

pepper to taste

1. Preheat oven to 400 degrees F. Place bread cubes on a baking sheet. Drizzle olive oil and butter on top and toss to coat. Sprinkle with salt.

2. Bake bread cubes for 8 to 10 minutes, flipping halfway through, until golden brown. Remove from oven and cool.

3. While bread bakes, prepare dressing. Whisk all dressing ingredients together in a small bowl.

4. In a large bowl, combine toasted bread cubes, tomatoes, cucumbers, bell pepper, red onion, and basil. Pour dressing on top and toss to coat. Add more salt and pepper to taste.

Sheet Pan Omelet

Prep: 10 minutes • Cook: 30 minutes • Serves 8

The amount of eggs we eat at our house is a little insane. Someone is always cooking eggs at some point in the day. The best thing about this sheet pan omelet is that you can customize toppings in sections to cater to everyone's likes and dislikes.

12 large eggs

½ cup milk or heavy cream

½ cup diced ham

1 cup diced bell pepper
   (any color)

¼ cup diced red onion

salt and pepper to taste

¾ cup shredded cheddar cheese

TOPPINGS

sour cream

salsa

1.Preheat oven to 350 degrees F. Spray a jelly roll pan with nonstick cooking spray or line with foil.

2. In a large bowl, whisk eggs and milk or cream together. Stir in ham, bell pepper, onion, and salt and pepper to taste. Pour mixture into prepared pan and sprinkle with cheddar cheese.

3. Bake for 20 to 30 minutes or until top is lightly browned and eggs are set. Cut into squares and serve immediately. Top with sour cream and salsa if desired.

SCRUMPTIOUS TIP

The protein in this recipe can easily be interchanged with cooked sausage or bacon.

Sheet Pan Philly Cheesesteak

Prep: 10 minutes • Cook: 25 minutes • Serves 6

My husband loves a good Philly cheesesteak sandwich. This version is made from what I usually have on hand, which is ground beef. Make sure you eat it on buttered and toasted rolls to get the full experience.

1 ½ pounds lean ground beef

6 ounces cream cheese, softened

2 teaspoons steak seasoning

2 teaspoons Worcestershire sauce

salt and pepper to taste

2 tablespoons olive oil

8 ounces white button mushrooms, sliced

3 cups sliced bell pepper (any color)

1 cup diced onion

8 ounces sliced or shredded provolone cheese

sliced rolls for serving

butter for rolls

mayonnaise for rolls

1. Preheat oven to 350 degrees F. Spray a jelly roll pan with nonstick cooking spray or line with foil.

2. In a large skillet, cook beef over medium-high heat until browned. Drain.

3. Add cream cheese, steak seasoning, and Worcestershire sauce. Cook over medium heat for 3 minutes or until cream cheese is melted and combined. Add salt and pepper to taste. Spread beef mixture on prepared sheet pan.

4. Wipe out skillet. Heat olive oil over medium-high heat. Add mushrooms, bell pepper, and onion. Cook until veggies are soft, adding more olive oil if needed.

5. Spread veggies on top of beef mixture. Top with provolone cheese. Bake for about 5 minutes or until cheese is melted.

6. Serve immediately on sliced, toasted rolls with butter and mayonnaise.

One-Pan Breakfast Bake

Prep: 5 minutes • Cook: 45 minutes • Serves 6

Imagine that you can cook all the breakfast things—the hash browns, the bacon, the eggs—at the same time. Genius, right?

1 (20-ounce) package frozen hash browns, thawed

2 tablespoons olive oil

1 teaspoon seasoned salt

pepper to taste

6 ounces bacon, cut into 1-inch-long slices

6 eggs

½ cup shredded cheddar cheese

1. Preheat oven to 400 degrees F. Line a 13x18-inch baking sheet with foil and spray with nonstick cooking spray.

2. Pour hash browns into pan. Drizzle with olive oil. Toss well with seasoned salt and pepper. Spread into an even layer on three-fourths of the pan.

3. Add bacon pieces to other side of pan. Bake for 30 to 35 minutes or until hash browns and bacon are browned and crispy.

4. Set aside bacon. Stir cooked hash browns and spread in an even layer over the whole pan. Sprinkle bacon on top.

5. Make 6 wells in hash browns. Carefully crack each egg into a well. Sprinkle hash browns with cheese. Bake for 5 to 7 minutes until whites are set or until desired doneness.

Honey Garlic Pork Roast

Prep: 5 minutes • Cook: 8 hours in slow cooker; 75 minutes in Instant Pot • Serves 10

This sweet and savory honey garlic pork roast can be cooked in a slow cooker or an Instant Pot. This can be prepped in less than five minutes, and the result is a tender, fall-apart pork roast that can be eaten plain or on a sandwich.

1 (3 to 4 pound) pork roast

1 or 2 cups low-sodium chicken broth

¼ cup balsamic vinegar

¼ cup soy sauce

2 tablespoons honey

2 teaspoons minced garlic

2 teaspoons cornstarch

SLOW COOKER

1. Place pork roast in slow cooker. Combine 1 cup chicken broth and remaining ingredients except cornstarch in a small bowl. Whisk together and pour over roast.

2. Cook on low for 10 to 12 hours or high for 6 to 8 hours.

3. Once roast is done, spoon out ¼ cup juice from slow cooker. Mix with cornstarch to make a slurry. Add more juice until you have about 1 cup. Heat on stove over medium heat, whisking until mixture thickens. Pour over pork right before serving.

INSTANT POT

1. Place pork roast in Instant Pot. Combine 2 cups chicken broth and remaining ingredients except cornstarch in a small bowl. Whisk together and pour over roast.

2. Rotate lid to locked position and set Instant Pot to Manual High Pressure for 1 hour 15 minutes. Let pressure release naturally when done.

3. Once roast is done, spoon out ¼ cup juice from Instant Pot. Mix with cornstarch to make a slurry. Add more juice until you have about 1 cup. Heat on stove over medium heat, whisking until mixture thickens. Pour over pork right before serving.

Chicken Cordon Bleu Pasta

Prep: 5 minutes • Cook: 60 minutes • Serves 12

This recipe makes enough to feed a crowd. This creamy pasta is made with chicken and ham in a cheesy sauce and topped with a crunchy panko topping.

16 ounces short pasta (trottole pictured)

4 tablespoons unsalted butter

¼ cup flour

4 cups milk

1 tablespoon Dijon mustard

1 teaspoon garlic powder

1 teaspoon salt

½ cup grated Parmesan cheese

1 ½ cups (6 ounces) shredded Swiss cheese, divided

2 cups shredded mozzarella cheese, divided

3 cups shredded rotisserie chicken

1 cup (8 ounces) diced ham

salt and pepper to taste

1 cup panko breadcrumbs

1. Preheat oven to 350 degrees F. Spray a 9x13-inch baking dish with nonstick cooking spray.

2. In a large pot, bring several cups salted water to a boil. Cook pasta al dente according to package directions. Do not overcook; pasta will continue to cook in the oven.

3. In a saucepan, melt butter over medium heat. Sprinkle flour on top and cook for 1 to 2 minutes or until mixture thickens.

4. Whisk in milk slowly. Add Dijon mustard, garlic powder, and salt. Simmer for 3 to 5 minutes, whisking constantly, until mixture thickens. Remove from heat. Stir in Parmesan cheese, 1 cup Swiss cheese, and 1 cup mozzarella cheese.

5. Once pasta is done, drain well. Pour pasta into cheese sauce. Add rotisserie chicken and ham. Stir together until combined. Season with salt and pepper to taste. Pour into prepared baking dish. Sprinkle with remaining cup mozzarella cheese.

6. In a small bowl, combine panko breadcrumbs and remaining ½ cup Swiss cheese. Sprinkle over casserole.

7. Bake uncovered for 30 to 40 minutes or until breadcrumbs are golden and casserole is bubbly.

Mini Chicken Chimichangas

Prep: 10 minutes • Cook: 20 minutes • Makes 16 chimichangas

These chimichangas are filled with creamy chicken and cheddar cheese. Eat them as an appetizer or a main meal. They're perfect for switching up Taco Tuesday!

8 ounces cream cheese, softened

1 tablespoon taco seasoning

2 cups shredded cheddar cheese

3 cups shredded rotisserie chicken

16 to 20 (6-inch) flour tortillas

1 tablespoon unsalted butter, melted

TOPPINGS

sour cream

guacamole

pico de gallo

1. Preheat oven to 350 degrees F. Line a baking sheet with parchment paper or spray with nonstick cooking spray.

2. In a large bowl, add cream cheese, taco seasoning, cheddar cheese, and chicken. Stir until well combined.

3. Place about ¼ cup chicken mixture in the center of a tortilla. Fold the sides in and roll the tortilla up. Place on baking sheet seam side down. Repeat for remaining tortillas and filling. Brush with melted butter.

4. Bake for 15 to 20 minutes or until chimichangas are golden brown and crispy.

5. Top with desired toppings, such as sour cream, guacamole, and pico de gallo.

Sheet Pan Pancakes

Prep: 5 minutes · Cook: 20 minutes · Serves 12

Instead of being held prisoner to the stovetop flipping pancakes, try this sheet pan version. Cut these fluffy pancakes into squares and serve with fresh fruit and whipped cream.

3 eggs

3 cups buttermilk

2 tablespoons sugar

1 teaspoon vanilla extract

2 ⅔ cups flour

2 teaspoons baking powder

1 teaspoon baking soda

1 teaspoon salt

6 tablespoons unsalted butter, melted

TOPPINGS

sliced fresh strawberries

fresh blueberries

maple syrup

whipped cream

1. Preheat oven to 500 degrees F. Line a 13x18-inch baking sheet with parchment paper and spray with nonstick cooking spray.

2. In a large bowl, whisk together eggs, buttermilk, sugar, and vanilla.

3. In a medium bowl, combine flour, baking powder, baking soda, and salt.

4. Stir buttermilk mixture into flour mixture. Stir in melted butter until just combined. Do not overmix.

5. Pour batter onto prepared baking sheet in an even layer.

6. Reduce oven temperature to 425 degrees F. Bake for 16 to 17 minutes or until toothpick comes out clean.

7. Cut into squares and serve with fruit, syrup, and whipped cream.

SCRUMPTIOUS TIP

The trick to getting the pancakes to rise is heating the oven really high initially. Then we reduce the temperature while baking so the pancakes don't dry out.

Creamy Italian Pasta Salad

Prep: 15 minutes • Cook: 10 minutes • Serves 10

I'm always looking for a go-to side for potlucks and barbecues. This pasta salad can be modified to use whatever veggies you like.

---

8 ounces small pasta shells

¾ cup chopped bell pepper (any color)

¾ cup grape tomatoes, quartered

½ cup chopped pepperoni

½ cup chopped salami

½ cup whole olives

2 ounces provolone cheese, cubed

¼ cup diced red onion

2 cups chopped romaine lettuce

DRESSING

⅓ cup olive oil

¼ cup red wine vinegar

2 tablespoons mayonnaise

2 tablespoons sugar

1 ½ teaspoons salt

1 ½ teaspoons dried oregano

½ teaspoon pepper

1. Cook pasta according to package directions. Drain and rinse in cold water.

2. While pasta cooks, prepare dressing. In a small bowl, whisk all dressing ingredients together.

3. Place pasta in a large bowl. Add remaining ingredients, except for lettuce. Pour dressing over pasta mixture and toss to coat. Cover and refrigerate until ready to serve. Prior to serving, toss with fresh lettuce.

Twice-Baked Potato Casserole

Prep: 15 minutes • Cook: 85 minutes • Serves 12

There's nothing better than a loaded baked potato as a side dish to a meal. I like this casserole because it feeds a crowd all in one dish. Great for potlucks!

6 pounds russet potatoes, washed (about 6 to 8 large potatoes)

2 tablespoons olive oil

kosher salt

¾ cup unsalted butter, softened

1 cup sour cream

1 cup whole milk

1 teaspoon seasoned salt

1 ½ cups shredded cheddar cheese, divided

8 ounces bacon, cooked and crumbled, divided

½ cup sliced green onion, divided

1. Preheat oven to 425 degrees F. Pierce potatoes 2 to 3 times each with a fork. Rub potatoes with olive oil and sprinkle with kosher salt. Bake for 45 to 60 minutes or until potatoes are fork-tender.

2. Reduce heat to 400 degrees F. Spray a 9x13-inch baking dish with nonstick cooking spray.

3. Slice potatoes in half lengthwise and scoop insides into a large bowl. Add butter, sour cream, whole milk, and seasoned salt. Mash potatoes using a potato masher.

4. Stir in 1 cup cheddar cheese, half of the bacon, and ¼ cup green onion. Spoon potato mixture into prepared pan.

5. Bake for 20 minutes. Top with remaining ½ cup cheese remaining bacon. Bake for 5 minutes or until cheese is m Sprinkle with remaining ¼ cup green onion and serve.

SCRUMPTIOUS

You can make this meal ahead of time up t
refrigerator. If making ahead of time, you mc
final bake time to 30 minutes so the casser
all the way.

Sheet Pan
Mac & Cheese

Prep: 5 minutes · Cook: 30 minutes · Serves 12

This dish has all the best parts of macaroni and cheese. You get that cheesy goodness, and since we're cooking it on a sheet pan, every bite has that crunchy crumb topping.

---

1 pound elbow macaroni

4 tablespoons unsalted butter

2 cloves garlic, minced

¼ cup flour

2 cups whole milk

1 cup heavy cream

2 teaspoons Dijon mustard

1 teaspoon paprika

salt and pepper to taste

4 cups shredded sharp cheddar cheese, divided

_p grated Parmesan cheese

panko breadcrumbs

1. Position cooking rack in upper third of oven. Preheat oven to 450 degrees F. Spray an 18x13-inch sheet pan with nonstick cooking spray.

2. Bring a large pot of heavily salted water to a boil. Cook pasta al dente according to package directions. Pasta will continue to cook in oven. Drain and set aside.

3. In a large saucepan, melt butter over medium-high heat. Add garlic and cook for 30 seconds. Sprinkle flour on top and cook for about 1 minute.

4. Slowly whisk in milk and cream. Stir in Dijon mustard and paprika. Cook until mixture thickens, about 4 minutes. Add salt and pepper to taste.

5. Remove from heat. Stir in 3 cups cheddar cheese, grated Parmesan cheese, and drained pasta until well combined. Pour into prepared pan in an even layer.

6. In a small bowl, combine panko breadcrumbs and remaining cup cheddar cheese. Sprinkle breadcrumb mixture on top of pasta.

7. Bake for 8 to 10 minutes or until cheese is bubbly and breadcrumbs are golden brown.

Overnight Breakfast Casserole

Prep: 15 minutes • Cook: 70 minutes • Additional: 4 hours chill time • Serves 12

My family loves having people come visit us, and I'm always brainstorming about what to feed them in the morning. I'm not a morning person, so the fact that this dish can be prepared the night before is a huge bonus. Layers of bread, crispy bacon, green onion, crunchy bell pepper, and cheesy eggs bake together to make a hearty breakfast.

12 slices white bread, cubed

10 slices bacon, cooked and crumbled

½ cup sliced green onion

½ cup finely diced red bell pepper

4 cups shredded cheddar cheese

6 eggs, lightly beaten

2 cups milk

½ teaspoon dry mustard

½ teaspoon salt

½ teaspoon black pepper

1. Spray a 9x13-inch baking dish with nonstick cooking spray.

2. In prepared baking dish, layer half the bread cubes, half the bacon, half the green onion, half the pepper, and 2 cups cheese. Repeat.

3. In a large bowl, whisk together eggs, milk, dry mustard, salt, and pepper. Pour mixture over casserole.

4. Cover and refrigerate overnight or for at least 4 hours to let milk soak into bread.

5. Remove casserole from refrigerator and let it sit on the counter while the oven preheats.

6. Preheat oven to 350 degrees F. Cover. Bake for 50 minutes. Uncover and bake for 15 additional minutes to let bread brown. Casserole is done when center is set and cooked. Bake longer if needed.

game-day eats

My husband, John, played for the Miami Dolphins for fourteen years. Football wasn't just a part of our life—it was our whole life. Each of my babies grew up in the stadium and took naps during the fourth quarter. Rain or shine, we were there. After the game, we always went home to eat a spread of our favorite game-day foods. To say that football food has a special place in our hearts is an understatement. All of my football memories are intertwined with the food we ate.

‹ Pizza Rolls P. 71

Cheesy Chicken Taquitos

Prep: 15 minutes • Cook: 20 minutes • Serves 16

I cook more than the average person, so there's always food up for grabs on my counter. Seeing what my neighbor kids and family eat first is an easy way to see what's popular. These cheesy chicken taquitos always go in minutes. They have a spicy, cheesy inside and a crispy baked tortilla outside.

2 cups shredded rotisserie chicken

1 ½ cups shredded Pepper Jack cheese

4 ounces cream cheese, softened

¼ cup salsa

2 tablespoons lime juice

½ teaspoon chili powder

½ teaspoon garlic powder

½ teaspoon ground cumin

½ teaspoon salt

16 (6-inch) flour tortillas

1 tablespoon unsalted butter, melted

kosher salt

TOPPINGS

sour cream

guacamole

pico de gallo

chopped cilantro

1. Preheat oven to 425 degrees F. Line a baking sheet with parchment paper.

2. In a medium bowl, combine chicken, Pepper Jack cheese, cream cheese, salsa, lime juice, chili powder, garlic powder, cumin, and salt.

3. Spread 2 tablespoons of filling on the lower third of a tortilla. Roll up tightly and place on baking sheet seam side down. Repeat with remaining tortillas and filling.

4. Brush tops of tortillas with butter and sprinkle with kosher salt.

5. Bake for 15 to 20 minutes or until taquitos are golden brown and crispy. Cut in half and top with sour cream, guacamole, pico de gallo, and chopped cilantro.

SCRUMPTIOUS TIP

A fun way to present this dish is in a two-layered ring that people can pull apart, as shown in the picture. To create the rings, cut the taquitos in half and layer in two circles before baking. Sprinkling an extra ½ cup cheese between the layers helps keep them together. Bake as directed.

Creamy Artichoke Dip

Prep: 10 minutes • Cook: 45 minutes • Serves 8

There's a good chance that if artichoke dip is on the menu at a restaurant, I will order it. My husband and I have become connoisseurs of the best artichoke dips around. Gruyére cheese is a little off the beaten path, but it adds a taste that no other cheese can match.

2 tablespoons unsalted butter

1 cup chopped yellow onion

4 cloves garlic, minced

2 tablespoons flour

1 cup heavy cream

1 cup grated Parmesan cheese, divided

2 (12-ounce) jars marinated artichoke hearts, drained and coarsely chopped

¼ cup sour cream

½ cup shredded Gruyère cheese, divided

½ cup shredded mozzarella cheese, divided

½ cup panko breadcrumbs

chips, sliced baguettes, or naan for dipping

1. Preheat oven to 375 degrees F. Spray a shallow 9-inch square baking dish with nonstick cooking spray

2. In a skillet, melt butter over medium-high heat. Add onion and sauté for a few minutes until soft. Add garlic and cook for 1 minute. Sprinkle with flour and cook for 1 minute.

3. Slowly whisk in cream and ¾ cup Parmesan cheese until sauce thickens slightly.

4. Stir in artichokes, sour cream, ¼ cup Gruyére cheese, and ¼ cup mozzarella cheese.

5. Pour mixture into prepared baking dish. Top with remaining ¼ cup Parmesan cheese, remaining ¼ cup Gruyère cheese, and remaining ¼ cup mozzarella cheese. Sprinkle panko breadcrumbs on top.

6. Bake for 30 to 35 minutes or until dip is bubbly and top is golden brown. Serve with chips, sliced baguettes, or naan.

Cheeseburger Sliders

Prep: 10 minutes • Cook: 30 minutes • Makes 24 sliders

These sliders may be simple, but they are always a crowd-pleaser. Just put seasoned beef with plenty of cheese in between dinner rolls. They're so simple to make and so delicious!

2 pounds lean ground beef

1 cup diced yellow onion

1 teaspoon salt

1 teaspoon pepper

1 teaspoon garlic powder

1 teaspoon Worcestershire sauce

¼ cup mayonnaise

24 small dinner rolls

12 ounces cheddar cheese, sliced or shredded

2 tablespoons unsalted butter, melted

1 tablespoon sesame seeds

1. Preheat oven to 350 degrees F. Spray a large baking sheet with nonstick cooking spray.

2. In a large skillet, add beef and onion. Cook and crumble beef until no longer pink. Drain. Stir in salt, pepper, garlic powder, Worcestershire sauce, and mayonnaise.

3. Slice rolls in half. Place bottom halves on prepared pan. Place half the cheese on rolls. Spoon beef on top in an even layer. Add remaining cheese and top with top halves of rolls. Brush buns with butter and sprinkle with sesame seeds.

4. Bake for 15 to 20 minutes or until sliders are golden brown and cheese is melted.

Totchos

Prep: 5 minutes • Cook: 50 minutes • Serves 8

Totchos, or tater tot nachos, are a switch-up on classic nachos. The possibilities of toppings are endless. Unlike nachos, these call for a fork. Make sure you get the tater tots nice and crispy before layering all of the toppings.

1 (32-ounce) package frozen tater tots

1 pound lean ground beef

⅔ cup water

1 (1-ounce) package taco seasoning

2 cups shredded cheddar cheese

TOPPINGS

guacamole

sour cream

pico de gallo

sliced green onion

1. Preheat oven to 425 degrees F.

2. Arrange tater tots in a single layer on a baking sheet. Bake for 25 to 35 minutes or until golden brown and crispy.

3. While tater tots cook, prepare taco meat. In a large skillet, brown beef until no longer pink. Add water and taco seasoning. Bring to a boil, then reduce heat. Simmer for 2 to 3 minutes or until mixture thickens and liquid is absorbed. Set aside until tater tots are ready.

4. When tater tots are ready, sprinkle taco meat and cheese on top. Bake for 3 to 5 minutes or until cheese is melted.

5. Top with desired toppings, such as guacamole, sour cream, pico de gallo, and green onion.

Pizza Rolls

Prep: 15 minutes • Cook: 20 minutes • Makes 8 rolls

We have pizza night every Friday night, and sometimes it's nice to switch things up. You can load these pizza rolls up with any toppings you like, but we love a classic pepperoni and sausage combo.

16 ounces pizza dough

¼ cup marinara sauce, plus more for dipping

1 cup pepperoni slices

½ cup cooked and crumbled Italian sausage

¼ cup grated Parmesan cheese

1 cup shredded mozzarella cheese, divided

GLAZE

2 tablespoons butter

½ teaspoon garlic powder

½ teaspoon Italian seasoning

pinch of salt

1. Preheat oven to 400 degrees F. Spray a 9-inch round baking dish with nonstick cooking spray.

2. On a lightly floured surface, roll out pizza dough to a 16x10-inch rectangle. Brush with marinara sauce, leaving a ½-inch margin on the edge.

3. Place pepperoni and sausage evenly on dough. Sprinkle with Parmesan cheese and ½ cup mozzarella cheese.

4. Roll up tightly, starting with long end. Pinch seam to seal. Cut into 8 slices and place in prepared dish.

5. Bake for 15 to 20 minutes or until center of rolls is cooked through.

6. Sprinkle remaining ½ cup mozzarella cheese on top and bake until melted.

7. In a small bowl, stir together glaze ingredients. Brush on top of cooked rolls.

8. Serve with warm marinara sauce for dipping.

Garlic Parmesan Wings

Prep: 40 minutes · Cook: 60 minutes · Serves 10

Our family likes our chicken wings extra crispy, and whenever we order them at a restaurant, they never come out crispy enough for our tastes. These chicken wings are a bit healthier because we bake them, not fry them. We use a special method to make them just as crispy!

2 pounds chicken wings

kosher salt

2 tablespoons baking powder

1 teaspoon garlic powder

blue cheese or ranch dressing
   for dipping

GARLIC PARMESAN SAUCE

¼ cup unsalted butter

4 cloves garlic, minced

pinch of red pepper flakes

2 tablespoons finely chopped
   flat-leaf parsley

4 tablespoons grated
   Parmesan, divided

1. Squeeze wings with paper towels to get out as much moisture as you can. Place on a baking sheet and sprinkle each wing with kosher salt. Let wings rest for 30 minutes. The salt draws out the moisture in the wings.

2. After 30 minutes, preheat oven to 250 degrees F. Spray a baking sheet with nonstick cooking spray.

3. Squeeze wings with paper towels again to get out the moisture. Place wings in a resealable plastic bag. Add baking powder and garlic powder to bag and shake to coat wings. Transfer wings to prepared baking sheet. Bake for 30 minutes.

4. Turn heat up to 450 degrees F. Cook for 20 to 30 minutes or until wings are at desired crispiness.

5. While wings bake, make the sauce. In a small skillet, melt butter over medium heat. Add garlic and red pepper flakes. Cook for 1 minute. Remove from heat. Stir in parsley and 2 tablespoons Parmesan.

6. Once wings are ready, toss in warm sauce. Sprinkle with remaining 2 tablespoons Parmesan cheese. Serve warm with blue cheese or ranch for dipping.

Creamy Queso

Prep: 5 minutes • Cook: 15 minutes • Serves 16

This queso can be made in minutes and feeds a crowd! We like to eat this with tortilla chips, but you can pour it on nachos, tacos, burritos, or enchiladas.

8 ounces Pepper Jack cheese, cubed

8 ounces Colby-Jack cheese, cubed

8 ounces cream cheese, softened

1 (10-ounce) can RO*TEL diced tomatoes and green chiles, drained

½ cup whole milk or heavy cream, plus more if needed

1 teaspoon garlic powder

1 teaspoon onion powder

1 teaspoon chili powder

1. In a medium saucepan, heat all ingredients on low, stirring occasionally, until combined. Do not use high heat or cheese will get grainy.

2. Add more milk or cream to desired consistency.

3. Eat with tortilla chips.

SCRUMPTIOUS TIP

You can change out the cheeses for whatever flavors you like. Be wary of store-bought preshredded cheeses. They often are coated in substances that keep them from clumping together and also cause them to not melt as well as cheese off the block.

Cheese should never be heated at a high temperature; high temperatures cause cheese to separate or get grainy. Low and slow is the best way to heat this up.

Greek Nachos

Prep: 45 minutes • Serves 8

I always say that I was meant to be Greek. I have a huge family—eighty-three first cousins on my dad's side alone. We love getting together. It's always loud, chaotic, and entertaining. These Greek nachos have the Greek flavors I love, like feta, cucumber, olive, and red onion. The sauce is a fresh tzatziki. You can buy premade tzatziki sauce, but homemade is so much better when the time allows.

6 cups pita chips

1 cup tzatziki

½ cup hummus

1 medium cucumber, diced

1 cup cherry tomatoes, quartered

½ cup crumbled feta cheese

¼ cup kalamata olives

¼ cup diced red onion

TZATZIKI

½ cup plain Greek yogurt

½ cup grated cucumber, liquid squeezed out with a towel

1 tablespoon extra-virgin olive oil

1 tablespoon fresh dill, minced

1 tablespoon lemon juice

1 tablespoon red wine vinegar

2 cloves garlic, minced

¼ teaspoon kosher salt, plus more to taste

pepper to taste

1. For the tzatziki sauce, combine all ingredients. Let mixture chill in refrigerator for at least 20 minutes.

2. For the nachos, layer pita chips on a serving dish. Top with remaining ingredients. Serve immediately.

Jalapeño Popper Bread

Prep: 10 minutes • Cook: 20 minutes • Serves 16

I love eating jalapeño poppers, but they are a lot of work to make. This version has all of the "stuff" that a jalapeño popper has but piled on top of a loaf of French bread. You might never go back to regular jalapeño poppers.

1 loaf French bread

8 ounces cream cheese, softened

1 cup shredded mozzarella cheese

1 cup shredded cheddar cheese

4 slices bacon, cooked and crumbled

2 jalapeños, seeded and diced

2 tablespoons mayonnaise

1 tablespoon garlic powder

1. Preheat oven to 400 degrees F.

2. Cut French bread in half lengthwise and place both pieces open-faced on a baking sheet.

3. In a medium bowl, mix remaining ingredients until well combined. Spread half on each slice of bread.

4. Bake for 15 minutes. Turn heat up to broil and cook for a few additional minutes, until cheese starts to brown. Cool slightly, then slice and serve.

SCRUMPTIOUS TIP

I've learned this the hard way, but it's important to wash your hands right after handling jalapeños because the juice can irritate your skin. Also make sure to keep your hands away from your face and eyes. Even better, wear gloves when working with jalapeños.

Cuban Sandwich Dip

Prep: 5 minutes • Cook: 20 minutes • Serves 10

My family lived in south Florida for fifteen years, and Floridians are known for their Cuban sandwiches. I thought to myself, "Why not turn a Cuban sandwich into a dip?"

8 ounces diced ham

8 ounces cream cheese, softened

8 ounces (2 cups) shredded Swiss cheese

3 tablespoons dill pickles, finely diced

3 tablespoons yellow mustard

3 tablespoons mayonnaise

crackers, chips, or sliced baguettes for dipping

1. Preheat oven to 350 degrees F. Spray a 9-inch round or square baking dish with nonstick cooking spray.

2. In a large bowl, mix all ingredients except crackers until well combined. Pour into prepared baking dish.

3. Bake for 10 to 15 minutes until bubbly. Turn heat up to broil and cook for 2 to 3 minutes or until cheese starts to brown. Serve with crackers, chips, or sliced baguettes.

Brown Sugar Smokies

Prep: 15 minutes • Cook: 35 minutes • Serves 12

These brown sugar smokies are a mix of savory and sweet. These couldn't be easier to make, and there are enough for a crowd!

1 pound bacon

1 (16-ounce) package
   Lit'l Smokies sausages

toothpicks

1 cup brown sugar

1. Preheat oven to 350 degrees F. Line a baking sheet with foil and spray with nonstick cooking spray.

2. Cut each piece of bacon into thirds. Wrap each sausage with a piece of bacon, securing with a toothpick. Bake for 20 minutes.

3. Sprinkle with brown sugar. Bake for 10 to 15 minutes or until bacon is cooked to desired crispiness and brown sugar is melted. Serve warm.

Italian Roll-Ups

Prep: 20 minutes • Makes 48 rolls

These Italian roll-ups are all of the layers of an Italian sandwich rolled up in a tortilla with cream cheese, peperoncini, and roasted red peppers. These always go fast!

8 ounces cream cheese, softened

¼ cup chopped peperoncini

¼ cup finely chopped roasted red peppers

1 teaspoon Italian seasoning

6 (8-inch) flour tortillas

18 slices salami

18 slices deli ham

30 pepperoni slices

12 slices provolone cheese

6 romaine lettuce leaves

¾ cup chopped tomato

toothpicks

1. In a medium bowl, combine cream cheese, peperoncini, roasted red peppers, and Italian seasoning until well blended. Spread about 3 tablespoons of mixture on each tortilla.

2. Layer 3 slices salami, 3 slices ham, 5 pepperoni, 2 slices provolone cheese, and a lettuce leaf on each tortilla, leaving a ½-inch margin on the edge. Sprinkle with a few chopped tomatoes.

3. Tightly roll up each tortilla. Pin shut with toothpicks about ¾ inch apart. Slice between toothpicks.

4. Refrigerate until ready to serve.

SCRUMPTIOUS TIP

Remember that sizes will differ, so all of these ingredients are approximate. You just want a layer of each ingredient per roll.

Warm BLT Dip

Prep: 10 minutes • Cook: 20 minutes • Serves 16

This dip can be thrown together in five minutes and ready for the opening kickoff. You can't really go wrong with a warm, creamy dip that has bacon, tomatoes, and green onion in it.

1 cup mayonnaise

1 cup sour cream

8 ounces cream cheese, softened

1 pound bacon, cooked and crumbled

1 ½ cups shredded cheddar cheese

1 tomato, seeded and chopped

¼ cup sliced green onion

TOPPINGS

cooked bacon

tomato

green onion

lettuce

corn chips or sliced baguettes for serving

1. Preheat oven to 350 degrees F.

2. Mix mayonnaise, sour cream, and cream cheese in a bowl until thoroughly combined. Crumble bacon into mixture and stir. Add cheddar cheese, tomato, and green onion. Mix well.

3. Pour into a shallow dish or pie pan. Bake for 20 minutes or until bubbly.

4. Garnish with additional bacon, tomato, green onion, and lettuce. Serve with corn chips or sliced baguettes.

SLOW COOKER

1. Add all ingredients and mix together. Cook on low for 2 hours. You can keep warm in slow cooker until serving.

SCRUMPTIOUS TIP

Make sure to squeeze the tomato before chopping to rid it of any excess juice so that you don't have unnecessary liquid in your dip.

low-carb favorites

These recipes are low-carb and keto-friendly, but they use normal ingredients, so they won't scare off an unsuspecting friend or neighbor. My husband, John, deserves credit for this section because he spent so much time creating and testing these low-carb recipes to make sure they were just right.

‹ Million-Dollar Chicken P. 115

Mushroom Risotto

Prep: 5 minutes • Cook: 15 minutes • Serves 8

This low-carb cauliflower mushroom risotto will give your regular old risotto a run for its money. This decadent side dish is substantial enough to be an entrée.

4 tablespoons unsalted butter

8 ounces sliced white mushrooms, coarsely chopped

½ cup diced white onion

2 cloves garlic, minced

1 cup low-sodium chicken broth

12 ounces frozen or fresh riced cauliflower

¾ cup heavy cream

1 cup grated Parmesan cheese

¼ teaspoon salt

¼ teaspoon pepper

chopped parsley for garnish

1. In a large skillet, melt butter over medium-high heat. Add mushrooms and onion. Cook until veggies are tender, about 5 minutes. Add garlic and cook for an additional 30 seconds.

2. Add chicken broth, riced cauliflower, and cream. Simmer until liquid is reduced to desired consistency, about 10 minutes. Stir in Parmesan, salt, and pepper. Top with parsley.

SCRUMPTIOUS TIP

If you use frozen riced cauliflower, you may need to simmer the risotto longer to reduce the liquid.

This can be turned into a meal by adding your choice of protein, such as chicken or shrimp.

Buffalo Chicken Salad

Prep: 15 minutes • Serves 6

If there is any way to make a Buffalo version of a recipe, I will try to do it! My husband's side of the family is obsessed with all things Buffalo flavored. Turns out, a classic chicken salad tastes great with a Buffalo twist.

3 cups shredded rotisserie chicken

½ cup mayonnaise

½ cup finely diced celery

¼ cup Buffalo wing sauce

¼ cup sliced green onion

½ teaspoon kosher salt

lettuce leaves for serving (optional)

½ cup blue cheese crumbles for topping (optional)

1. In a medium bowl, combine all ingredients except lettuce leaves and blue cheese crumbles. Chill in refrigerator until serving.

2. Serve plain or in lettuce leaves. Top each serving with blue cheese crumbles if desired.

Carne Asada

Prep: 10 minutes • Cook: 20 minutes • Marinade: 4 to 12 hours • Serves 8

Carne asada is well-seasoned meat marinated in bright citrus flavors and grilled. This dish is great all by itself or on a salad, in tacos, in burritos, or on nachos.

1 jalapeño, seeded and diced

½ cup diced white onion

½ cup chopped cilantro

¼ cup fresh orange juice

¼ cup fresh lime juice

¼ cup olive oil

¼ cup soy sauce

2 tablespoons white vinegar

1 teaspoon kosher salt

1 teaspoon ground black pepper

1 teaspoon garlic powder

1 teaspoon chili powder

1 teaspoon dried oregano

1 teaspoon ground cumin

4 cloves garlic, minced

2 pounds flank steak

tortillas for serving (optional)

TOPPINGS

sour cream

guacamole

pico de gallo

1. In a medium bowl, whisk together all ingredients except for steak. Place steak in a baking dish and pour marinade on top. Let steak marinate in refrigerator for 4 to 12 hours.

2. Preheat grill to medium-high heat and oil grate. Remove steak from refrigerator and discard marinade. Grill steak for 6 to 8 minutes on each side or until it reaches desired doneness. Let meat rest for 5 minutes before slicing.

3. Slice steak thinly against the grain into strips or cubes. Serve plain or in tortillas. Top with guacamole, sour cream, or pico de gallo if desired.

SCRUMPTIOUS TIP

I love the flavor grilling gives this dish, but if the grill is intimidating, this can be cooked in a skillet on the stove.

Egg Roll in a Bowl

Prep: 5 minutes • Cook: 15 minutes • Serves 4

This is hands down the most popular low-carb recipe on my blog, so I wanted to include it here. Egg roll in a bowl is a one-pan dinner made in fifteen minutes. It's packed with protein and flavor. Made with either ground pork or beef, this keto-friendly recipe tastes just like an Asian egg roll without the egg roll wrapper.

1 pound ground pork or beef

1 teaspoon minced garlic

14 ounces coleslaw mix or shredded cabbage

¼ cup low-sodium soy sauce or liquid aminos

1 teaspoon ground ginger

1 egg

2 teaspoons sriracha

1 tablespoon sesame oil

2 tablespoons sliced green onion

1. In a large skillet, brown meat until no longer pink. Drain.

2. Add garlic and sauté for 30 seconds. Add coleslaw or cabbage, soy sauce or liquid aminos, and ginger. Sauté until desired tenderness.

3. Make a well in the center of the skillet. Add egg. Scramble over low heat until done.

4. Stir in sriracha. Drizzle with sesame oil and sprinkle with green onion. Add additional soy sauce and sriracha if desired.

Creamy Parmesan Shrimp

Prep: 5 minutes • Cook: 10 minutes • Serves 4

This creamy Parmesan shrimp comes together in less than ten minutes and tastes like it could be from a restaurant. I always prefer fresh shrimp, but frozen can be used as well.

2 tablespoons unsalted butter

1 ½ pounds shrimp, peeled and deveined

½ teaspoon kosher salt

1 tablespoon minced garlic

½ cup heavy cream

¼ cup grated Parmesan cheese

salt and pepper to taste

parsley for garnish

1. In a large skillet, melt butter over medium-high heat. Season shrimp with kosher salt. Add shrimp to skillet. Cook for 3 to 4 minutes or until shrimp are pink and not translucent. Transfer shrimp to a plate and cover.

2. Add garlic to skillet. Cook for 30 seconds. Add cream. Bring to a simmer. Cook for about 1 minute.

3. Add shrimp back to skillet. Stir in Parmesan cheese and add salt and pepper to taste. Sprinkle with parsley and serve immediately.

Low-Carb Biscuits and Gravy

Prep: 10 minutes • Cook: 30 minutes • Makes 9 Biscuits

If you're craving biscuits and gravy without all the carbs, I promise that this recipe will give you your fix. Thick cheddar biscuits smothered in a creamy sausage gravy are the ultimate comfort food.

BISCUITS

2 large eggs

2 tablespoons cottage cheese or sour cream

2 tablespoons unsalted butter, melted

1 cup almond flour

½ teaspoon baking powder

¼ teaspoon Himalayan pink salt or sea salt

1 cup shredded cheddar cheese

GRAVY

½ pound pork breakfast sausage

8 ounces cream cheese, softened

1 cup low-sodium chicken broth

salt and pepper to taste

1. Preheat oven to 400 degrees F. Line a baking sheet with parchment paper.

2. In a medium bowl, whisk together eggs, cottage cheese or sour cream, and butter. Set aside.

3. In a separate bowl, whisk together almond flour, baking powder, and salt. Add dry ingredients to wet ingredients and stir to combine. Mixture will be wet. Stir in cheddar cheese.

4. Drop batter onto prepared baking pan in dollops, about 3 tablespoons each. Bake for 12 to 14 minutes or until biscuits turn golden brown.

5. While biscuits bake, make gravy. In a large skillet, cook and crumble sausage until browned. Add cream cheese and chicken broth. Heat over medium-high heat until mixture has thickened. Add salt and pepper to taste.

6. To serve, pour warm gravy over biscuits.

Italian Spinach Salad

Prep: 15 minutes • Serves 4

If you need a quick, healthy lunch, this Italian spinach salad can be whipped up in minutes. Its light, tangy dressing complements the tomatoes, mozzarella, pepperoni, and salami.

3 cups baby spinach, roughly chopped

2 cups grape tomatoes, halved

8 ounces small fresh mozzarella balls

½ cup chopped pepperoni

½ cup chopped salami

¼ cup red onion, chopped finely

DRESSING

¼ cup olive oil

2 tablespoons lemon juice

½ teaspoon Italian seasoning

pinch of salt

1. In a salad bowl, combine all salad ingredients.

2. In a small bowl, whisk together all dressing ingredients.

3. Toss salad with dressing right before serving. Add more salt and pepper to taste.

SCRUMPTIOUS TIP

You can buy mozzarella balls at the store labeled as bocconcini or mozzarella pearls. Likewise, a block of mozzarella cheese can be cubed as a substitute.

Rueben Hot Pockets

Prep: 20 minutes • Cook: 15 minutes • Serves 4

My husband loves a good Reuben sandwich so much that he came up with a low-carb version to satisfy his craving.

FATHEAD DOUGH

1 ½ cups shredded mozzarella cheese

1 ounce cream cheese, softened

¾ cup almond flour

1 large egg

½ teaspoon salt

FILLING

4 ounces corned beef

4 slices Swiss cheese

½ cup sauerkraut, thoroughly drained

THOUSAND ISLAND DRESSING

½ cup mayonnaise

2 tablespoons sugar-free tomato ketchup

2 tablespoons chopped dill pickle

2 tablespoons minced white onion

1 tablespoon apple cider vinegar

1 tablespoon low-carb powdered sugar

1 teaspoon Worcestershire sauce

pinch of salt and pepper

1. Preheat oven to 400 degrees F. Line a baking sheet with parchment paper.

2. Heat mozzarella and cream cheese in microwave in 30-second intervals, just until cheeses melt and you are able to mix them together.

3. Add almond flour, egg, and salt. Stir until well combined with a dough-like consistency. If it is too sticky, you can add a little more almond flour. As the dough cools, it will become easier to manage.

4. Roll out dough between two pieces of parchment paper on a large baking sheet. You want to form a roughly 10x14-inch rectangle. Cut into fourths.

5. Divide meat, cheese, and sauerkraut equally between each section of dough, leaving a ½-inch margin on the edge. Fold dough over filling and press edges together to seal.

6. Bake for 10 to 15 minutes on prepared baking sheet until golden brown.

7. While pockets cook, prepare dressing. Mix all dressing ingredients and chill in refrigerator until ready to serve.

8. Serve finished pockets with Thousand Island dressing.

SCRUMPTIOUS TIP

A classic Rueben is made from corned beef, but you could use pastrami or ham as a substitute.

Creamy Bacon Mushroom Chicken

Prep: 15 minute • Cook: 40 minutes • Serves 6

In this low-carb recipe, we combine chicken in a creamy mushroom sauce with crispy bacon on top. This restaurant-worthy dish all happens in one pan and can be made in thirty minutes or less.

---

2 tablespoons olive oil

2 pounds boneless skinless chicken thighs or breasts

salt and pepper

8 ounces bacon, chopped

½ cup diced onion

8 ounces sliced mushrooms

4 cloves garlic, minced

2 cups heavy cream

1 cup low-sodium chicken broth

1 tablespoon Dijon mustard

1 teaspoon dried thyme

1 teaspoon dried rosemary

¼ cup grated Parmesan cheese

chopped basil for garnish

1. In a large skillet, heat olive oil over medium-high heat. Season chicken thighs with salt and pepper. Cook chicken for 4 to 6 minutes on each side or until chicken is no longer pink. Remove chicken and set aside.

2. Add bacon to skillet and cook until crispy. Drain on paper towels. Reserve about 2 tablespoons bacon grease in pan and discard the remainder.

3. In the same pan with bacon grease, cook onion and mushrooms over medium-high heat until soft. Add garlic and cook for an additional minute.

4. Add cream, chicken broth, Dijon mustard, thyme, and rosemary. Simmer for 5 to 7 minutes or until sauce thickens. Stir in Parmesan cheese.

5. Add chicken back to pan. Heat through and sprinkle with bacon. Top with chopped basil. Serve.

French Toast Custard

Prep: 10 minutes • Cook: 10 minutes • Serves 4

The hardest thing about eating low-carb is satisfying your sweet tooth. This French toast custard is so easy (almost too easy) and tastes like it sounds, like French toast meets custard.

4 large eggs

½ cup water

½ cup heavy cream

3 tablespoons zero-carb sweetener (e.g., monkfruit, erythritol)

1 teaspoon vanilla

⅛ teaspoon salt

TOPPINGS

cinnamon

whipped cream

sugar-free syrup

berries

1. Stir eggs, water, and cream together in a bowl with a fork until smooth. Add sweetener, vanilla, and salt. Place mixture in a wide shallow bowl that will fit in the container of your Instant Pot.

2. Fill bottom of Instant Pot with approximately 1 inch water. Cover bowl with tin foil and lower into Instant Pot with a rack.

3. Pressure-cook on low for 10 minutes. When done, manually release pressure.

4. Add your choice of toppings and enjoy.

SCRUMPTIOUS TIP

For this recipe, the key is a 1:1 ratio of eggs to liquid. Four eggs equals 1 cup, so can use any combination of 1 cup liquid. For example, if you want a rich, creamy custard, you could use 1 cup heavy cream. For a reduced-calorie custard, use almond or coconut milk.

If you don't have an Instant Pot, you can make this in the oven. Just place the bowl of custard in a water bath and bake at 350 degrees F for 30 minutes or until custard is set.

Parmesan Brussels Sprouts

Prep: 10 minutes • Cook: 25 minutes • Serves 4

Does it mean that I'm actually an adult now that I crave foods like brussels sprouts? The Parmesan coats the brussels sprouts and makes them extra crispy, just how I like them.

1 pound brussels sprouts, halved

4 ounces bacon, finely chopped

3 tablespoons olive oil

½ cup grated Parmesan cheese

3 cloves garlic, minced

½ teaspoon Italian seasoning

½ teaspoon kosher salt

1. Preheat oven to 400 degrees F. Line a sheet pan with parchment paper.

2. In a large bowl, toss brussels sprouts and bacon in olive oil. Stir in remaining ingredients.

3. Spread mixture on prepared sheet pan, making sure to turn brussels sprouts cut side down. Bake for 15 to 20 minutes or until brussels sprouts are at desired tenderness and bacon is crispy.

SCRUMPTIOUS TIP

Turning the brussels sprouts so they are cut side down is a little more work, but it's worth it. This helps them get extra crispy!

Tuscan Soup

Prep: 10 minutes • Cook: 20 minutes • Serves 6

The flavors of Tuscany are all in this easy, low-carb soup. My family gobbles this one up!

1 pound mild Italian sausage

½ cup diced yellow onion

4 cloves garlic, minced

6 cups low-sodium chicken broth

½ cup sun-dried tomatoes, drained and chopped

1 teaspoon dried oregano

2 cups kale or spinach, coarsely chopped

¾ cup heavy cream

salt and pepper to taste

grated Parmesan for topping

1. In a large pot, brown sausage over medium-high heat. Drain.

2. Add onion and cook for a few minutes until soft. Add garlic and cook for an additional minute.

3. Stir in chicken broth, tomatoes, and oregano. Bring mixture to a simmer.

4. Stir in kale and heavy cream. Add salt and pepper to taste. Sprinkle with Parmesan for serving.

Million-Dollar Chicken

Prep: 5 minutes • Cook: 40 minutes • Serves 4

The reason this chicken has a million-dollar name is that it's rich and decadent.

1 ½ pounds boneless skinless chicken breasts, thinly cut

salt and pepper

6 ounces cream cheese, softened

½ cup cooked and crumbled bacon

½ cup chopped green onion

¼ cup mayonnaise

1 ½ cups shredded Colby–Jack cheese, divided

1. Preheat oven to 350 degrees F. Place chicken breasts in a baking dish and season with salt and pepper.

2. In a medium bowl, combine cream cheese, bacon, green onion, mayonnaise, and ¾ cup cheese. Spread mixture on top of chicken. Top with remaining ¾ cup cheese.

3. Cover with foil and bake for 30 to 40 minutes, until chicken is no longer pink. Remove foil for last 10 minutes of baking so cheese can melt. Serve.

SCRUMPTIOUS TIP

A pair of good kitchen scissors comes in handy to cut thick chicken breasts in half lengthwise to create thin chicken breasts. Thin chicken breasts make the chicken-to-topping ratio more even for this recipe.

Low-Carb Turtles

Prep: 5 minutes • Cook: 10 minutes • Makes 12 turtles

I like to keep these low-carb turtles in the refrigerator for a quick sweet tooth fix. Not only are these easy to make, but the flavors are so complementary.

¼ cup unsalted butter

2 tablespoons granulated low-carb sweetener (e.g., erythritol, allulose)

¼ cup heavy cream

1 teaspoon vanilla extract

2 cups whole pecans, coarsely chopped

½ cup low-carb chocolate chips or chocolate salted caramel baking chips (e.g., Lily's)

sea salt for topping (optional)

1. In a large saucepan, melt butter and sweetener over medium-high heat for 4 to 5 minutes, stirring occasionally, until sauce turns golden brown.

2. Stir in cream. Remove from heat. Stir in vanilla extract and chopped nuts.

3. Place scoops (about 3 tablespoons each) on a parchment-lined baking sheet. Place in freezer while melting chocolate.

4. In a microwave-safe bowl, melt chocolate in 30-second intervals, stirring in between.

5. Remove turtles from freezer. Drizzle chocolate evenly on top. Immediately top with sea salt if desired.

Egg Salad BLT

Prep: 15 minutes • Cook: 15 minutes • Serves 4

A creamy egg salad between two halves of a chaffle make for a very tasty lunch or dinner. You can keep the egg salad in the refrigerator for a quick snack.

CHAFFLES

4 large eggs

2 cups shredded cheddar cheese

EGG SALAD

4 hard-boiled eggs, coarsely chopped

3 tablespoons mayonnaise

¼ cup chopped celery

2 tablespoons sliced green onion

1 teaspoon lemon juice

1 teaspoon yellow mustard

⅛ teaspoon salt

⅛ teaspoon pepper

ADDITIONAL SANDWICH TOPPINGS

sliced tomato

sliced avocado

bacon

lettuce

1. To prepare chaffles, mix eggs with cheese. Cook in a mini waffle iron. This should yield 8 chaffles.

2. In a large bowl, combine all egg salad ingredients. Stir together gently.

3. Place your egg salad with desired toppings between two chaffles and enjoy.

SCRUMPTIOUS TIP

What is a chaffle? It's a cheesy egg waffle that can easily substitute for bread.

Mini waffle irons sure are cute, but if you don't have one, just divide the batter into eighths and use a regular waffle iron.

Kielbasa Cabbage Skillet

Prep: 10 minutes • Cook: 25 minutes • Serves 6

This kielbasa cabbage skillet may not be very attractive to the eye, but once you taste it, none of that will matter. This low-carb dinner is filling.

2 tablespoons olive oil

¾ cup diced yellow onion

3 cloves garlic, minced

2 tablespoons white vinegar

1 (14-ounce) package kielbasa, thinly sliced

2 tablespoons unsalted butter

1 tablespoon Dijon mustard

1 head green cabbage, thinly sliced

½ teaspoon paprika

¼ teaspoon red pepper flakes

salt and pepper to taste

1. In a large skillet, heat olive oil over medium-high heat. Add onion and sauté for 4 to 6 minutes or until onion is soft. Add garlic and cook for an additional 30 seconds.

2. Stir in vinegar and add kielbasa. Cook for 4 to 6 minutes or until browned.

3. Add butter, Dijon mustard, and cabbage. Stir together well. Cook until cabbage gets tender, about 5 to 10 minutes.

4. Season with paprika, red pepper flakes, and salt and pepper to taste. Serve immediately.

Enchilada Meatza

Prep: 20 minutes · Cook: 30 minutes · Serves 6

If pizza and enchiladas had a baby, you'd get this high-protein Mexican dinner. Low-carb and full of flavor, this dinner is a winner!

CRUST

2 (10-ounce) cans chunk chicken, drained

½ cup shredded cheddar cheese

2 large eggs

1 tablespoon taco seasoning

MEAT

½ pound ground beef

¼ cup chopped white onion

½ tablespoon taco seasoning

5 ounces enchilada sauce

1 ½ cups preshredded Mexican blend cheese

TOPPINGS

sour cream

guacamole

tomatoes

black olives

cilantro

enchilada sauce

1. Preheat oven to 350 degrees F. Line a baking sheet with parchment paper.

2. Spread chicken on a separate baking sheet. Bake for 10 to 12 minutes to dry out the chicken.

3. While chicken dries out, prepare meat. In a large skillet, cook ground beef, onion, and taco seasoning over medium-high heat. Once beef is cooked, turn off heat and stir in enchilada sauce.

4. Remove chicken from oven. Turn oven up to 500 degrees F. Place chicken in a bowl and mix in cheese, eggs, and taco seasoning.

5. Place dough on prepared baking sheet in 6 equal portions. Use a second piece of parchment paper on top to help roll out piles into flat, thin crusts. Bake crusts for 8 to 10 minutes.

6. Add ground beef on top of crusts and sprinkle each with ¼ cup cheese. Bake for 5 minutes or until cheese melts. Top with desired toppings.

quick and easy

We all want a pile of recipes that can be made with few ingredients at a moment's notice. Here's a stack of my go-to quick and easy recipes for all occasions.

‹ Chicken Tortellini with Asparagus P. 128

Barbecue Chicken Pizza

Prep: 10 minutes • Cook: 15 minutes • Serves 6

Six ingredients are all you need to make this barbecue chicken pizza, which is kid-friendly (minus the green things) but also nice enough for a date night in.

1 (13.8-ounce) package refrigerated or homemade pizza dough

1 cup chopped rotisserie chicken

½ cup barbecue sauce, divided

2 cups shredded mozzarella cheese

⅓ cup sliced red onion

2 tablespoons chopped cilantro leaves

1. Preheat oven to 500 degrees F. Line a baking sheet with parchment paper.

2. Roll out pizza dough on floured surface to desired shape. Transfer to baking sheet.

3. In a small bowl, combine chicken and ¼ cup barbecue sauce. Set aside.

4. Brush dough with remaining ¼ cup barbecue sauce, leaving a ½-inch border. Sprinkle mozzarella cheese on pizza and top with barbecue chicken and red onion.

5. Bake for 10 to 12 minutes or until crust is golden brown. Sprinkle with chopped cilantro.

Chicken Tortellini with Asparagus

Prep: 10 minutes • Cook: 20 minutes • Serves 4

If you're looking for a quick weeknight meal done in less than 20 minutes, this chicken tortellini with asparagus fits the bill. Although the ingredients are simple, the basil and sun-dried tomatoes are flavor-packed and add a vibrant taste.

9 ounces refrigerated cheese tortellini

2 tablespoons olive oil

1 pound boneless skinless chicken breasts, chopped

salt and pepper

½ cup sun-dried tomatoes, drained and chopped, divided

1 pound asparagus, trimmed into 2½-inch pieces

½ cup basil pesto

1 cup grape tomatoes, halved

1. Cook tortellini according to package directions. Drain.

2. While tortellini cooks, heat olive oil in a large skillet. Season chicken with salt and pepper. Add chicken and ¼ cup sun-dried tomatoes to pan. Cook chicken over medium-high heat for 5 to 7 minutes or until chicken is no longer pink. Remove chicken and tomatoes from pan and set aside.

3. Add remaining ¼ cup sun-dried tomatoes and asparagus to pan. Season with salt and pepper. Cook on medium-high heat for 5 to 7 minutes or until asparagus is tender. Reduce heat to low.

4. Add tortellini and cooked chicken and tomatoes to pan. Toss with basil pesto and stir in grape tomatoes. Add salt and pepper to taste. Serve.

Strawberry Feta Walnut Salad

Prep: 10 minutes • Cook: 5 minutes • Serves 4

This is one of those salads that looks like you spent a long time making it but that you can throw together in minutes. The sweetness of the crunchy candied walnuts with the tang of the crumbled feta cheese and fresh strawberries makes this salad craveable.

CANDIED WALNUTS

½ cup sugar

1 cup walnuts

SALAD

4 cups spinach

2 tablespoons balsamic vinegar

1 tablespoon olive oil

2 cups strawberries, sliced

½ cup crumbled feta cheese

salt and pepper to taste

1. In a small skillet, melt sugar over medium heat for a few minutes. As soon as sugar melts, toss in walnuts. Pour onto parchment to cool. When cooled, break into pieces.

2. In a bowl, toss together spinach, balsamic vinegar, and olive oil.

3. Add strawberries, feta, and walnuts. Add salt and pepper to taste. Toss and serve immediately.

Beef and Broccoli

Prep: 10 minutes • Cook: 30 minutes • Serves 4

This easy beef and broccoli is for those busy nights when dinner has to be quick. The beef is marinated in brown sugar and soy sauce and then baked with broccoli for a well-rounded meal.

1 ½ pounds beef sirloin, New York strip, or tenderloin, cut into 1-inch chunks

4 tablespoons reduced-sodium soy sauce, divided

3 tablespoons brown sugar, divided

4 cups broccoli florets

1 tablespoon sesame oil

3 cloves garlic, minced

1 teaspoon freshly grated ginger

¼ teaspoon crushed red pepper flakes

salt and pepper to taste

sliced green onion for garnish

sesame seeds for garnish

1. Preheat oven to 425 degrees F. Spray a baking sheet with nonstick cooking spray.

2. In a large bowl, combine steak, 2 tablespoons soy sauce, and 1 tablespoon brown sugar. Let marinate for 5 minutes.

3. Arrange steak and broccoli in a single layer on prepared baking sheet. Bake for 15 to 20 minutes, until steak is cooked and broccoli is tender.

4. In a small saucepan, combine remaining 2 tablespoons soy sauce, 2 tablespoons brown sugar, sesame oil, garlic, ginger, and red pepper flakes. Bring mixture to a boil. Reduce heat to a simmer and cook for a few minutes, until mixture has thickened.

5. Drizzle mixture over steak and broccoli. Add salt and pepper to taste. Garnish with green onion and sesame seeds.

Creamy Chicken Soup

Prep: 10 minutes • Cook: 15 minutes • Serves 6

Utah is known for its snow. On a really snowy day, all I want to do is hunker down with a comfy blanket and some of this warm creamy chicken soup.

2 tablespoons olive oil

¾ cup diced carrot

½ cup diced yellow onion

½ cup diced celery

2 cloves garlic, minced

5 to 6 cups low-sodium chicken broth

1 ½ cups ditalini pasta, uncooked

8 ounces cream cheese, softened

½ cup heavy cream

½ teaspoon thyme

½ teaspoon kosher salt

2 cups shredded rotisserie chicken

chopped parsley for garnish

1. In a large pot, heat olive oil over medium-high heat. Add carrot, onion, and celery. Cook for 5 to 6 minutes or until veggies are soft. Add garlic and cook for an additional minute.

2. Add chicken broth, pasta, cream cheese, heavy cream, thyme, and salt. Bring mixture to a boil. Reduce heat to medium and cook for 5 to 7 minutes or until pasta is tender.

3. Stir in rotisserie chicken and season with more salt and pepper as needed. Garnish with chopped parsley and serve.

SCRUMPTIOUS TIP

Most grocery stores sell mirepoix—which is prediced onion, carrot, and celery all ready to go for soups—in their produce section. Mirepoix is a great time-saver if you're in a hurry.

Monterey Chicken Quesadillas

Prep: 10 minutes • Cook: 15 minutes • Serves 4

Have you ever baked quesadillas? Baking gives them a crunch that is so good! These Monterey chicken quesadillas are stuffed with barbecue chicken, cheddar cheese, bacon, and green onion for a flavorful quick dinner.

1 cup shredded rotisserie chicken

2 cups shredded cheddar cheese

⅓ cup barbecue sauce

4 slices bacon, cooked and crumbled

2 tablespoons green onion

2 tablespoons unsalted butter, softened

4 (8-inch) flour tortillas

chopped tomatoes for garnish (optional)

1. Preheat oven to 400 degrees F.

2. In a large bowl, combine chicken, cheddar cheese, barbecue sauce, bacon, and green onion.

3. Butter one side of a tortilla and place it butter side down on a baking sheet. Spread a quarter of the mixture on half of the tortilla. Fold the other half over. Repeat with remaining filling and tortillas.

4. Bake for 5 to 6 minutes, then flip and bake for another 5 to 6 minutes until tortillas are slightly brown. Slice and serve with chopped tomatoes.

Ham and Egg Breakfast Braid

Prep: 10 minutes • Cook: 35 minutes • Serves 10

This ham and egg breakfast braid looks really impressive but is actually so easy. It's a crescent dough braid stuffed with cheesy scrambled eggs. Slice it up to serve.

8 large eggs

¼ cup milk

2 tablespoons sliced green onion

1 tablespoon unsalted butter

2 (8-ounce) cans refrigerated crescent dough sheets

¼ pound sliced deli ham

¾ cup shredded cheddar cheese

1. Preheat oven to 375 degrees F. Line a large baking sheet with parchment paper.

2. In a medium bowl, whisk together eggs and milk. Reserve about 2 tablespoons mixture in a separate small bowl and set aside. Stir green onion into remaining egg mixture.

3. In a large skillet, melt butter over medium heat. Add egg mixture. Cook until just done. Season with salt and pepper.

4. Unroll crescent dough sheets onto prepared baking sheet. Place long sides of sheets next to each other. Press or roll crescent dough together with your fingers or a rolling pin to create a large rectangle.

5. Layer ham down center of rectangle. Top with scrambled egg mixture and shredded cheese.

6. Cut 1-inch slits in the dough down both sides. Starting at the top, fold each strip over the egg mixture, alternating sides, to braid.

7. Brush reserved egg mixture over dough. Bake for 30 to 35 minutes or until braid is golden brown and center is fully cooked.

Basil Parmesan Salmon

Prep: 5 minutes • Cook: 15 minutes • Serves 4

Your family will be shocked at how few ingredients are in this basil parmesan salmon. The creamy topping helps keep the salmon from getting dry and has a bright herb flavor.

---

4 (approximately 5-ounce) salmon fillets

½ lemon, juiced (about 2 tablespoons)

kosher salt and ground black pepper

¼ cup mayonnaise

¼ cup shredded Parmesan cheese

2 tablespoons finely chopped basil leaves

1. Preheat oven to 425 degrees F. Line a baking sheet with parchment paper or spray with nonstick cooking spray.

2. Place salmon fillets on prepared baking sheet. Squeeze lemon juice on top of each fillet. Season with salt and pepper.

3. In a small bowl, combine mayonnaise, Parmesan cheese, and basil. Spread mixture evenly on fillets.

4. Bake for 12 to 15 minutes, depending on the thickness of the salmon, until salmon flakes easily with a fork.

Ham, Sweet Potato, and Kale Skillet

Prep: 5 minutes • Cook: 15 minutes • Serves 4

This ham, sweet potato, and kale skillet is a great way to use up leftover ham. Spinach can easily replace the kale in a pinch. The sweet potatoes paired with the savory ham make this dish a hit!

1 tablespoon olive oil

½ cup diced white onion

2 cloves garlic, minced

¾ cup low-sodium chicken broth, plus more as needed

2 ½ cups peeled and cubed sweet potato

1 ½ cups diced ham

2 cups kale, chopped

1 cup cheddar cheese, divided

1. In a large skillet, heat olive oil over medium-high heat. Add onion. Sauté until tender. Add garlic and cook an additional 30 seconds.

2. Add chicken broth and sweet potato. Cover. Simmer over low heat 8 to 10 minutes, until sweet potato is tender. Add more chicken broth as needed if liquid evaporates.

3. Stir in ham and kale. Cook until kale is tender. Add salt and pepper to taste.

4. Stir in ½ cup cheese. Sprinkle remaining ½ cup cheese on top. Cover and let cheese melt. Serve.

Healthy Cookie Dough Balls

Prep: 15 minutes • Makes 12 balls

My mom used to make peanut butter, oat, and honey balls for me after school growing up. This version is a little more indulgent with some added chocolate chips. A little chocolate never hurt anyone.

1 cup oat flour

½ cup natural peanut butter

3 tablespoons honey

1 tablespoon coconut oil, melted

1 teaspoon vanilla extract

½ cup semisweet chocolate chips

In a large bowl, mix all ingredients together well. Form 12 balls. Store in refrigerator.

SCRUMPTIOUS TIP

If you don't have oat flour, you can make your own. Add some oats to a blender or food processor and blend until oats are fine.

Prosciutto Asparagus Bundles

Prep: 15 minutes • Cook: 15 minutes • Makes 12 bundles

Mix only six ingredients and you have an elegant appetizer on the table. Layers of butter puff pastry wrap asparagus and prosciutto with melted Gruyére cheese.

2 sheets frozen puff pastry, thawed

16 ounces asparagus, ends trimmed

1 tablespoon olive oil

kosher salt and pepper

12 slices prosciutto

8 ounces Gruyére cheese, shredded

1 large egg, beaten

1. Preheat oven to 425 degrees F. Line a baking sheet with parchment paper.

2. Roll out puff pastries on a lightly floured surface into large rectangles. Cut each rectangle into 6 squares (12 squares total).

3. In a medium bowl, toss asparagus in olive oil and season with salt and pepper.

4. On each pastry square, layer 1 slice prosciutto, 2 to 3 stalks of asparagus diagonally, and about 2 tablespoons cheese. Fold two opposing corners of dough over asparagus, pressing together. Brush tops of dough with egg.

5. Bake for 12 to 15 minutes or until bundles are golden brown. Serve immediately.

Crispy Chickpea, Avocado, Tomato, and Feta Salad

Prep: 15 minutes • Cook: 5 minutes • Serves 4

This vegetarian side dish is zesty and savory all in one. Crispy seasoned chickpeas are tossed with avocados, fresh tomatoes, cilantro, and feta. Add a squeeze of lime to brighten it up!

2 tablespoons olive oil

1 (15-ounce) can chickpeas, drained, rinsed, and patted dry

2 cloves garlic, minced

¼ teaspoon paprika

salt and pepper

2 avocados, diced

⅓ cup grape tomatoes, halved

⅓ cup chopped cilantro

⅓ cup crumbled feta

¼ cup sliced green onion

1 lime, juiced (about 1 tablespoon juice)

1. In a skillet, heat olive oil over medium-high heat. Add chickpeas. Cook for 4 to 5 minutes or until crisp. Add garlic and paprika. Season with salt and pepper. Cook for an additional 30 seconds. Let chickpeas cool.

2. In a medium bowl, add avocados, grape tomatoes, cilantro, feta, and green onion. Gently toss with lime juice and season with salt and pepper. Stir in cooled chickpeas. Best served immediately.

tried and true

These are the recipes that have been made a hundred times. The recipe cards are stained and splashed with abundant use and memories of my childhood. These are the comfort foods: the recipes your grandma made, the soups your mom made when you were sick, the Sunday dinners you enjoyed around the table while talking with your loved ones.

‹ White Chicken Enchiladas P. 154

Stuffed Shells

Prep: 15 minutes • Cook: 30 minutes • Makes 24 shells

These stuffed shells are filled with a generous amount of cheese and are the ultimate comfort food. This recipe makes enough for two pans: one pan to eat and one to freeze for a rainy day.

8 ounces jumbo dried pasta shells (about 24 shells)

2 cups whole-milk ricotta cheese

2 cups shredded mozzarella cheese, divided

½ cup grated Parmesan, plus more for topping

1 large egg

1 teaspoon garlic powder

1 tablespoon flat-leaf parsley, chopped, or 1 teaspoon dried parsley

½ teaspoon salt

2 cups marinara sauce, divided

1. Preheat oven to 350 degrees F. Spray a 9x13-inch baking dish with nonstick cooking spray.

2. In a large pot of heavily salted water, cook pasta al dente. Drain and cool.

3. In a medium bowl, combine ricotta, 1 cup mozzarella, Parmesan, egg, garlic powder, parsley, and salt.

4. Pour 1 cup marinara on bottom of prepared baking dish. Spoon a heaping tablespoon of filling into each cooled pasta shell. Place seam side up in marinara. Pour remaining cup marinara sauce on top. Sprinkle with remaining cup mozzarella cheese.

5. Cover and bake for 15 minutes. Uncover and bake for 5 minutes or until cheese is bubbly. Sprinkle with additional Parmesan cheese and serve.

SCRUMPTIOUS TIP

I always cook a few extra pasta shells just in case some tear while boiling.

White Chicken Enchiladas

Prep: 10 minutes • Cook: 30 minutes • Makes 8 enchiladas

These white chicken enchiladas are a classic Mexican dish that everyone should have in their back pocket. Cheesy chicken is rolled in tortillas and baked in a creamy white sauce. Of course, no enchilada is complete without all of the toppings!

2 cups shredded rotisserie chicken

2 cups shredded Monterey Jack cheese, divided

salt and pepper

8 (8-inch) flour tortillas

3 tablespoons unsalted butter

3 tablespoons flour

1 ½ cups low-sodium chicken broth

1 cup sour cream

1 (4-ounce) can diced green chiles

TOPPINGS

guacamole

sour cream

pico de gallo

1. Preheat oven to 350 degrees F. Spray a 9x13-inch baking dish with nonstick cooking spray.

2. In a medium bowl, mix chicken and 1 cup Monterey Jack cheese. Season with salt and pepper. Spoon mixture evenly into tortillas and roll up tightly. Place seam side down in prepared dish.

3. In a skillet, melt butter over medium-high heat. Sprinkle flour over butter and cook for 1 minute.

4. Whisk in chicken broth. Simmer until mixture thickens, about 3 minutes. Remove from heat. Stir in sour cream and green chiles.

5. Pour sauce over tortillas. Sprinkle with remaining cup cheese.

6. Bake for 20 to 25 minutes. Then broil for a few minutes to brown cheese. Serve with desired toppings, such as guacamole, sour cream, and pico de gallo.

Homemade Chicken Noodle Soup

Prep: 50 minutes • Cook: 25 minutes • Serves 6

This homemade chicken noodle soup recipe is a tried-and-true comfort dinner with carrots, celery, onion, chicken, and homemade noodles. Once you see how easy it is to make homemade noodles, it's hard to go back to store-bought.

EGG NOODLES

1 ¼ cups flour

pinch of salt

1 egg, beaten

¼ cup milk

½ tablespoon unsalted butter, softened

SOUP

2 tablespoons unsalted butter

¾ cup chopped onion

¾ cup chopped celery

1 cup sliced carrots

2 cloves garlic, minced

9 cups low-sodium chicken broth

2 cups uncooked egg noodles (store-bought or homemade)

½ teaspoon dried basil

½ teaspoon dried oregano

dash of poultry seasoning (optional)

salt and pepper to taste

2 cups cooked and shredded chicken breast

1. In a large bowl, stir together flour and salt. Add beaten egg, milk, and butter. Knead dough until smooth, about 5 minutes. Let rest in a covered bowl for 10 minutes.

2. On a floured surface, roll out to ⅛- or ¼-inch thickness. Cut into desired lengths and shapes. Separate and allow to air-dry before cooking. For best results, let air-dry for a couple of hours, but 30 minutes will do.

3. When noodles are dry, prepare soup. In a large pot over medium heat, melt butter. Add onion, celery, and carrots and cook until just tender, about 5 minutes. Add garlic and cook for an additional minute.

4. Pour in chicken broth. Stir in noodles, basil, oregano, poultry seasoning (optional), and salt and pepper to taste. Bring to a boil. Reduce heat and simmer for 15 to 20 minutes.

5. Stir in chicken. Cook until heated through. Serve.

Chicken Parmesan Meatballs

Prep: 20 minutes • Cook: 35 minutes • Makes 20 meatballs

These chicken Parmesan meatballs are an Italian dinner that's ready in no time at all. Panko breadcrumbs give these seasoned meatballs that chicken Parmesan crunch. Serve these over noodles with garlic bread and a salad for a delicious dinner.

1 pound ground chicken

1 egg

½ cup grated Parmesan cheese

1 ¼ cups panko breadcrumbs, divided

1 teaspoon garlic powder

1 teaspoon Italian seasoning

1 teaspoon kosher salt

½ teaspoon pepper

½ teaspoon crushed red pepper flakes

4 tablespoons olive oil, divided

1 (26-ounce) jar marinara sauce

½ cup shredded mozzarella

2 tablespoons basil, torn (optional)

1. In a large bowl, mix chicken, egg, Parmesan cheese, ½ cup breadcrumbs, garlic powder, Italian seasoning, salt, pepper, and red pepper flakes. Roll into 1½-inch balls. Roll meatballs in remaining ¾ cup breadcrumbs.

2. In a large oven-safe skillet, heat 2 tablespoons oil over medium heat. Brown half of the meatballs on each side. Wipe out excess breadcrumbs. Repeat with remaining 2 tablespoons oil and remaining meatballs. Remove from pan and set aside.

3. Preheat oven to 350 degrees F. Pour marinara sauce in oven-safe skillet. Place meatballs on top of sauce.

4. Bake for 15 minutes. Sprinkle with mozzarella. Bake for 5 minutes. Garnish with basil and serve over pasta.

SCRUMPTIOUS TIP

If you don't have an oven-safe skillet, brown meatballs in a skillet, then transfer to an oven-safe baking dish.

Sometimes bits of the panko breadcrumbs fall off and start to burn in the oil, which is why we brown the meatballs in batches, wiping out the pan in between.

Garlic Knots

Prep: 2 hours 25 minutes • Cook: 15 minutes • Makes 16 rolls

There are few things better than a warm piece of buttery bread. I've been known to go to restaurants just for their bread baskets, so a good roll means a lot to me. These knots are fluffy and soft with a garlic butter glaze. We like to dip these in warm marinara sauce.

KNOTS

⅓ cup warm water (105 to 115 degrees F)

1 (.75-ounce) package active dry yeast (2 ¼ teaspoons)

1 ⅓ cups milk

6 tablespoons butter, softened

¼ cup sugar

1 large egg

2 teaspoons salt

4 to 5 cups flour

BUTTER GLAZE

2 tablespoons unsalted butter

½ teaspoon garlic powder

½ teaspoon dried parsley

pinch of salt

2 tablespoons grated Parmesan cheese for topping

1. In a small bowl, combine water and yeast. Let mixture sit for 5 minutes or until yeast reacts and is foamy.

2. Add yeast mixture to the bowl of a stand mixer or a large bowl if mixing by hand. Add milk, butter, sugar, egg, and salt. Mix until combined.

3. Slowly add 4 cups flour, mixing until combined. With mixer on low, gradually add up to 1 more cup flour, a little at a time, until dough pulls away from the sides of the bowl and forms a ball. You may not need all of the flour. Let mixer knead dough until smooth and elastic, about 5 minutes.

4. Cover dough and let rise in a warm place for about 1 hour until doubled in size.

5. Punch down dough and place on a floured surface. Divide dough in half. Then divide each half into 8 dough balls (16 balls total).

6. Roll each dough ball into a long rope about 9 inches long and tie in a knot. Line a baking sheet with parchment paper. Place knots on baking sheet and cover with a kitchen towel. Let knots rise for about 1 hour until doubled in size.

7. Preheat oven to 350 degrees F. Bake knots for 10 to 12 minutes or until barely brown.

8. While rolls bake, make garlic butter glaze. In a small bowl, microwave 2 tablespoons butter. Add garlic powder, parsley, and salt. Stir together.

9. Brush tops of warm rolls with butter glaze. Sprinkle with Parmesan cheese.

Banana Muffins

Prep: 15 minutes • Cook: 20 minutes • Makes 10 muffins

These banana muffins are moist with a little cinnamon and nutmeg and topped with tons and tons of crumb topping. This is the best way to use up ripe bananas.

BATTER

1 ½ cups flour

1 teaspoon baking soda

1 teaspoon baking powder

½ teaspoon salt

3 bananas, mashed (about 1 ½ cups)

¾ cup white sugar

1 egg, lightly beaten

⅓ cup unsalted butter, melted

1 teaspoon vanilla extract

1 teaspoon ground cinnamon

½ teaspoon ground nutmeg

CRUMB TOPPING

½ cup brown sugar

¼ cup flour

½ teaspoon ground cinnamon

2 tablespoons unsalted butter

1. Preheat oven to 375 degrees F. Line a muffin tray with 10 lightly greased reusable baking cups, or line a muffin tray with disposable paper baking cups.

2. In a large bowl, mix flour, baking soda, baking powder, and salt. In another bowl, beat together bananas, sugar, egg, butter, vanilla, cinnamon, and nutmeg. Stir banana mixture into flour mixture until just moistened. Spoon batter into prepared baking cups.

3. In a small bowl, mix brown sugar, flour, and cinnamon. Using two forks, a pastry blender, or your hands, cut in butter until mixture resembles wet sand. Sprinkle topping over muffins.

4. Bake for 15 to 20 minutes until a toothpick comes out clean.

Salmon Fresca

Prep: 10 minutes • Cook: 20 minutes • Serves 4

This salmon was inspired by a meal at a local Italian restaurant. The first time I made it, the flavors were magical, and I immediately put this recipe in my tried-and-true file. Fresh salmon topped with tomatoes, a balsamic glaze, and feta sits on top of a basil vinaigrette.

---

4 (approximately 5-ounce) salmon fillets

kosher salt and ground black pepper

2 tablespoons unsalted butter

2 tablespoons olive oil

1 cup spinach

2 tablespoons chopped basil

VINAIGRETTE

5 tablespoons basil pesto

1 tablespoon red wine vinegar

TOPPINGS

¼ cup chopped grape tomatoes

2 tablespoons crumbled feta cheese

balsamic glaze

1. Season salmon fillets with salt and pepper.

2. In a large skillet, heat butter and olive oil over medium-high heat. Add salmon. Cook for 5 to 7 minutes on each side or until desired doneness. Transfer to a plate and cover with foil to keep warm.

3. Prepare vinaigrette. In a small bowl, stir together basil pesto and red wine vinegar. Add 1 tablespoon vinaigrette to a medium skillet and set the rest aside.

4. Add spinach and basil to skillet with vinaigrette. Cook over medium heat for 2 to 3 minutes or until spinach starts to wilt.

5. To serve, spoon 1 tablespoon vinaigrette on each plate. Place warm salmon on top. Place ¼ of the spinach mixture on top of the salmon. Sprinkle with about 1 tablespoon chopped tomato and ½ tablespoon feta cheese on each fillet. Drizzle with balsamic glaze.

Chicken and Dumplings

Prep: 15 minutes • Cook: 25 minutes • Serves 8

If you've never had a dumpling, you've never experienced one of life's greatest pleasures. There's something so comforting about this delicious dish.

2 tablespoons unsalted butter

½ cup diced carrot

½ cup diced celery

½ cup diced yellow onion

3 cups shredded or cubed
   cooked chicken

8 cups low-sodium
   chicken broth

DUMPLINGS

2 cups flour

½ teaspoon baking powder

¼ teaspoon salt

2 tablespoons cold unsalted
   butter, cubed

1 cup milk

1. In a large pot, melt butter over medium-high heat. Add carrot, celery, and onion. Sauté until vegetables are soft, about 6 minutes. Add chicken and chicken broth. Bring to a simmer.

2. While chicken broth comes to a simmer, make dumplings. In a medium bowl, add flour, baking powder, and salt. Cut in cold butter with two forks, a pastry cutter, or your hands. Add milk and mix until combined.

3. On a floured surface, roll out dough to ¼-inch thickness. Cut dough into squares and toss with additional flour so pieces don't stick together.

4. Stir dumplings into chicken broth a few at a time. Simmer for about 15 minutes or until dumplings have cooked. Add more salt and pepper to taste. Serve.

The Best Crepes

Prep: 65 minutes · Cook: 15 minutes · Makes 16 crepes

My family loves crepes so much that I can't cook them fast enough! This tried-and-true recipe has the perfect consistency for a light crepe with filling.

4 eggs

2 ¼ cups milk

2 cups flour

1 tablespoon sugar

4 tablespoons unsalted butter, melted, plus more for cooking

1 teaspoon vanilla extract

¼ teaspoon salt

1. In a blender, combine all ingredients and blend until there aren't any lumps. Refrigerate for 1 hour to allow mixture to expand and absorb flour. Mixture can be refrigerated for up to 2 days.

2. In a skillet, melt a little butter over medium heat. Pour about ¼ cup crepe batter in the middle and swirl around. Cook until crepe is not shiny. Flip and cook other side. Repeat with remaining batter.

3. Serve with syrup, fruit, or powdered sugar.

SCRUMPTIOUS TIP

In full disclosure, I don't always refrigerate the batter for an hour before using. Although that's ideal, I've cooked them right away without issue.

169

Easy Bolognese

Prep: 15 minutes • Cook: 45 minutes • Serves 8

Nothing smells better than coming home to a Bolognese sauce simmering on the stovetop. The veggies are cooked into submission so that they blend in with the sauce. Your kids won't even know they're in there.

2 tablespoons olive oil

¼ cup finely diced onion

¼ cup finely diced carrot

¼ cup finely diced celery

2 cloves garlic, minced

½ pound ground beef

½ pound ground pork

½ teaspoon kosher salt, plus more to taste

ground black pepper

1 (26-ounce) jar marinara sauce

½ teaspoon dried basil

½ teaspoon dried oregano

½ cup heavy cream

cooked pasta for serving

Parmesan cheese for serving

1. In a large saucepan, heat oil over medium-high heat. Sauté onion, carrot, and celery until soft. Add garlic and cook an additional minute.

2. Add beef and pork. Season with salt and pepper. Cook until browned.

3. Pour in marinara sauce, basil, and oregano. Simmer on low for at least 30 minutes. Stir in cream.

4. Serve over cooked pasta and sprinkle with Parmesan cheese.

SCRUMPTIOUS TIP

Make a double batch and freeze half for a busy night. This sauce will freeze for up to 2 months.

Chicken, Spinach, and Potatoes

Prep: 15 minutes • Cook: 60 minutes • Serves 6

This chicken, spinach, and potatoes dish screams "Sunday dinner." Chicken and potatoes topped with a garlic Parmesan cream sauce make this a comfort meal that everyone loves.

3 cups peeled and diced Russet or Yukon Gold potatoes (these don't have to be peeled)

6 boneless skinless chicken thighs

kosher salt and freshly ground black pepper to taste

3 tablespoons unsalted butter, divided

3 cups baby spinach, roughly chopped

GARLIC PARMESAN CREAM SAUCE

¼ cup unsalted butter

4 cloves garlic, minced

2 tablespoons flour

1 cup low-sodium chicken broth

½ teaspoon dried thyme

1 teaspoon dried rosemary

½ cup heavy cream

½ cup grated Parmesan cheese

kosher salt and freshly ground black pepper to taste

1. Preheat oven to 400 degrees F. Spray a 9x13-inch baking dish with nonstick cooking spray.

2. Place potatoes in an even layer on bottom of prepared pan and season with salt and pepper

3. Season chicken with salt and pepper.

4. In a large skillet, melt 2 tablespoons butter over medium-high heat. Add chicken. Cook for 2 to 3 minutes, browning each side. Chicken will continue to cook in oven. Place on top of potatoes.

5. Melt remaining tablespoon butter in skillet. Add spinach. Cook for about 2 minutes or until spinach wilts. Add salt to taste. Place spinach in pan between chicken. Set pan aside.

6. Prepare garlic Parmesan sauce. In a skillet, melt butter over medium heat. Add garlic and cook for about 1 minute. Stir in flour and cook for 1 to 2 minutes.

7. Slowly whisk in chicken broth, thyme, and rosemary. Stir in cream and Parmesan. Cook for 2 to 3 minutes or until sauce thickens. Add salt and pepper to taste.

8. Pour sauce over chicken. Cover with foil and bake for 35 to 45 minutes or until potatoes are tender and chicken is no longer pink. Serve warm.

Butter Swim Biscuits

Prep: 15 minutes · Cook: 30 minutes · Makes 9 biscuits

These are called butter swim biscuits because the biscuits swim in a generous amount of butter while baking. The result? A thick Southern-style biscuit with a soft inside and a flaky crust. Eat them with jam, honey, or . . . you guessed it, more butter.

½ cup unsalted butter, melted

2 ½ cups flour

4 teaspoons baking powder

4 teaspoons sugar

1 teaspoon salt

1 ¾ cups buttermilk

1. Place a drip pan or baking sheet in oven under rack where baking dish will go to catch any butter that could spill over. Preheat oven to 450 degrees F.

2. Pour butter in a 9-inch square baking dish or a comparably sized dish.

3. In a large bowl, whisk together flour, baking powder, sugar, and salt. Stir in buttermilk until well combined. Dough will be wet.

4. Spread dough on top of butter as evenly as you can. Cut dough into 9 squares.

5. Bake for 20 to 25 minutes or until biscuits are golden brown and centers are cooked.

SCRUMPTIOUS TIP

To make homemade buttermilk, add 1 tablespoon lemon juice or white vinegar to 1 cup milk. Let mixture sit for 5 minutes until it starts to react, and you're done. For this recipe, you would need just shy of 2 tablespoons with 1 ¾ cups milk.

Broccoli Cheese Soup

Prep: 10 minutes • Cook: 35 minutes • Serves 6

I once had to make five different kinds of soup for a group of 250 women. Guess which soup disappeared the fastest? This one! This broccoli cheese soup is an easy, comforting soup that is hard to stop eating because it's so good.

¼ cup unsalted butter

½ medium onion, chopped

¼ cup flour

2 cups half-and-half cream

2 cups low-sodium
    chicken broth

½ pound broccoli, chopped into
    bite-size pieces (about 3
    cups)

1 cup matchstick carrots

salt and pepper

2 cups shredded sharp cheddar
    cheese

¼ teaspoon nutmeg (optional)

crusty bread for serving

1. In a large pot or saucepan, melt butter over medium heat. Sauté onions until soft. Sprinkle with flour. Stir and cook for 1 to 2 minutes.

2. Whisk in half-and-half and chicken broth. Add broccoli and carrots. Reduce heat to low. Cook for 20 to 25 minutes or until broccoli and carrots are tender.

3. Add salt and pepper. You can leave the soup chunky, or, for a smoother soup, you can blend about 1 cup soup and stir it back in.

4. Return to low heat. Add cheese. If your heat is too high when you add cheese, your soup can get grainy. Stir in nutmeg if desired.

5. Serve with crusty bread.

Shepherd's Pie

Prep: 15 minutes • Cook: 30 minutes • Serves 10

Shepherd's pie is one of the first meals I made when I went to college. It holds a special place in my heart for when I found my love of cooking.

1 pound lean ground beef

1 tablespoon olive oil

¾ cup diced onion

½ cup diced celery

2 cloves garlic, minced

2 tablespoons flour

2 tablespoons tomato paste

1 ¼ cups low-sodium beef broth

1 teaspoon dried parsley

½ teaspoon dried thyme

½ teaspoon dried rosemary

1 cup frozen peas and carrots

salt and pepper to taste

4 cups mashed potatoes

¾ cup shredded cheddar cheese

1. Preheat oven to 350 degrees F.

2. In a large skillet, brown beef over medium-high heat until no longer pink. Drain. Add olive oil, onion, and celery. Sauté until veggies are soft. Add garlic and cook an additional 30 seconds.

3. Sprinkle flour over beef and veggies. Add tomato paste. Cook for about 1 minute. Stir in beef broth. Add parsley, thyme, rosemary, and peas and carrots. Cook for 2 to 3 minutes over medium-high heat or until mixture thickens. Add salt and pepper to taste.

4. Pour into an 11x17-inch baking dish. Spoon mashed potatoes on top. Bake for 15 minutes.

5. Sprinkle with cheese. Bake for 5 minutes or until cheese melts. Serve.

something sweet

My friends always tell me that I have the biggest sweet tooth of anyone they know. I take that as a compliment! I really do believe that there is a second stomach for dessert, and no matter how full I am, I always find room for something sweet.

‹ Raspberry Cream Cheese Puffs P. 194

Birthday Cake Cinnamon Rolls

Prep: 2 hours • Cook: 20 minutes • Makes 12 rolls

Cinnamon rolls are one of my favorite desserts of all time, and I always make them on special occasions. They are definitely a labor of love with all of the rising, rolling, and cutting. Want to know a secret? You can totally cut a little of the prep work by starting with a cake mix. Don't knock it until you've tried it. This birthday cake version is magical, with rainbow sprinkles popping out of the cinnamon roll center.

DOUGH

1 ¼ cups warm water (105 to 115 degrees F)

1 (.75-ounce) package active dry yeast (2 ¼ teaspoons)

1 (15.25-ounce) package yellow cake mix

2 to 3 cups flour

FILLING

¼ cup butter, softened

½ cup brown sugar

1 teaspoon ground cinnamon

2 tablespoons rainbow sprinkles, plus more for topping

FROSTING

¼ cup unsalted butter, softened

4 ounces cream cheese, softened

2 cups powdered sugar

½ teaspoon vanilla extract

1 tablespoon milk

1. Spray a 9x13-inch baking dish with nonstick cooking spray.

2. In a small bowl, combine warm water and yeast. Let mixture stand for 5 minutes until mixture gets foamy.

3. In a large bowl, add cake mix and 2 cups flour. Mix in yeast mixture. Add up to 1 more cup flour a little at a time until dough pulls away from sides of bowl and forms a ball. You may not need to add all of the flour.

4. Once mixture is in a ball, cover with a kitchen towel and let rise in a warm place for about 1 hour until doubled in size.

5. Roll dough into a large rectangle, about 18x10 inches.

6. Brush softened butter on dough. In a small bowl, combine brown sugar and cinnamon. Sprinkle brown sugar mixture and rainbow sprinkles on butter.

7. Roll up jelly roll style, starting with long end. Slice into 12 rolls and place in prepared pan. Cover with a kitchen towel and let rise in a warm place for 30 minutes.

8. While rolls rise, preheat oven to 350 degrees F and prepare frosting. In a medium bowl, beat butter and cream cheese until fluffy. Add powdered sugar, vanilla, and milk. Mix slowly at first, then increase speed until fluffy. Add more milk if needed.

9. Bake rolls for 15 to 20 minutes or until tops are golden brown. Let cool 5 minutes before frosting.

10. Frost cinnamon rolls and sprinkle with rainbow sprinkles.

SCRUMPTIOUS TIP

You may be tempted to add sprinkles to the actual dough, but add them just to the cinnamon center and on top. From experience, sprinkles in the dough creates an ugly mix of colors, not a magical rainbow.

Sheet Pan Apple Crisp

Prep: 15 minutes • Cook: 35 minutes • Serves 12

Let's be honest—the best part of an apple crisp is the crisp part. This sheet pan version of apple crisp has the perfect apple-to-crisp ratio in every bite. Serve warm with a big scoop of vanilla ice cream.

APPLE FILLING

3 pounds Gala, Fuji, Honeycrisp, or Granny Smith apples (about 8 medium apples or 8 cups)

1 tablespoon fresh lemon juice

¼ cup brown sugar

2 tablespoons unsalted butter, melted

1 teaspoon ground cinnamon

pinch of salt

TOPPING

2 cups old-fashioned rolled oats

1 ½ cups flour

1 ¼ cups brown sugar

1 teaspoon ground cinnamon

1 teaspoon kosher salt

14 tablespoons unsalted butter, melted

vanilla ice cream for serving

1. Preheat oven to 425 degrees F.

2. Peel, core, and slice apples into ¼-inch-thick slices. Toss with remaining filling ingredients.

3. Place apple slices on an 18x13-inch sheet pan and spread evenly in a single layer. Cover with foil. Bake for 20 minutes or until apples are slightly soft.

4. While apples cook, prepare topping. In a large bowl, combine oats, flour, brown sugar, cinnamon, and salt. Add butter and stir until well combined.

5. When apples finish, sprinkle with topping. Bake uncovered for 15 minutes until topping is golden brown. Serve warm with vanilla ice cream.

Easy Blueberry Cobbler

Prep: 5 minutes • Cook: 45 minutes • Serves 8

This may be one of the easiest desserts you ever make. Stir, pour, and bake! I used blueberries here, but you can use any berry you like.

½ cup unsalted butter, melted

1 cup flour

1 cup sugar

1 cup milk

1 ½ cups blueberries

1. Preheat oven to 375 degrees F. Spray a 10-inch oven-safe skillet or baking dish with nonstick cooking spray.

2. In a large bowl, stir together butter, flour, sugar, and milk. Pour into prepared pan. Sprinkle with blueberries.

3. Bake for 40 to 45 minutes or until top starts to turn golden brown. Serve warm with ice cream.

Sheet Pan Strawberry Shortcake

Prep: 20 minutes • Cook: 25 minutes • Serves 24

The only strawberry shortcake I ever had growing up was a boxed lemon cake with strawberries on top. I didn't mind at all, but I didn't realize until I was older that traditional strawberry shortcake has a biscuit base. This sheet pan version has a thick biscuit base topped with sweetened whipped cream and fresh strawberries. It is delicious!

SHORTCAKE

3 ½ cups flour

½ cup sugar

2 tablespoons baking powder

½ teaspoon salt

1 cup cold unsalted butter, cubed

2 large eggs

2 cups heavy cream

STRAWBERRIES

4 cups strawberries, hulled and sliced

¼ cup sugar

WHIPPED CREAM

2 cups heavy whipping cream

⅓ cup powdered sugar

1 teaspoon vanilla extract

1. Preheat oven to 400 degrees F. Place an empty bowl for whipped cream in refrigerator to chill.

2. In a large bowl, whisk together flour, sugar, baking powder, and salt. Using two forks, a pastry cutter, or your hands, cut butter into flour mixture until coarse crumbs form.

3. Stir in eggs and cream until a dough forms. Dough will be very wet.

4. Using floured hands, press dough evenly into a 15x10x1-inch baking sheet. Bake for 20 to 25 minutes or until top is golden brown. Cool completely.

5. While shortcake bakes, combine strawberries and sugar in a bowl. Chill in the fridge until ready to use. Strawberries will start to make a sauce as they sit.

6. When ready to serve, make whipped cream. In chilled bowl, beat whipped cream ingredients until soft peaks form. Spread on shortcake and top with strawberry mixture. Cut into slices and serve.

Cookie Butter Lava Cookies

Prep: 20 minutes • Cook: 15 minutes • Makes 24 cookies

My absolute favorite cookie is from our local cookie company. It has a gooey cookie-butter lava center. I decided that I needed to come up with my own version.

1 cup unsalted butter, softened

1 cup brown sugar

1 cup granulated sugar

1 teaspoon salt

½ teaspoon baking powder

½ teaspoon baking soda

1 teaspoon vanilla

2 eggs

3 ¼ cups cake flour

1 cup Biscoff cookie butter

crumbled Biscoff cookies for topping (optional)

1. Preheat oven to 350 degrees F. Line cookie sheets with parchment paper.

2. Cream together butter, sugars, salt, baking soda, and baking powder. Add vanilla and eggs. Mix well. Add flour and mix until just blended.

3. Using a cookie scoop, scoop dough into 2-inch balls. Flatten balls into discs. Spoon about 1 teaspoon cookie butter onto the center of each disc. Fold discs in half, wrapping around cookie butter. Roll each cookie into a ball. Place on prepared cookie sheets about 4 inches apart.

4. Bake for 10 to 12 minutes or until set. Cool completely.

5. After cookies have cooled, melt about ¼ cup Biscoff in a small microwave-safe bowl. Using a fork, drizzle melted cookie butter on top of cooled cookies. Sprinkle with crumbled Biscoff cookies if desired.

SCRUMPTIOUS TIP

CAKE FLOUR: I never have cake flour on hand, but you can easily make your own. 1 cup cake flour is equal to 1 cup regular all-purpose flour with 2 tablespoons of flour replaced with cornstarch. I take my measuring cup and put 2 tablespoons cornstarch in, and then I fill the rest of the cup with flour. For this recipe, do this 3 times, and then add the remaining ¼ cup all-purpose flour.

COOKIE BUTTER: What is cookie butter? Cookie butter is a spread made from ground-up spice cookies created in Europe called speculaas or speculoos. While cookie butter used to be obsolete and found only at specialty stores, now it's in most grocery stores right next to the peanut butter.

No-Churn Banana Pie Ice Cream

Prep: 15 minutes • Freeze: 8 hours • Serves 10

Making homemade ice cream can be a long, arduous process, but this no-churn version is so simple and easy. Think banana pie meets ice cream!

2 cups heavy cream

1 (14-ounce) can sweetened condensed milk

4 ounces cream cheese, softened

1 cup mashed banana

1 teaspoon vanilla

1 cup coarsely crushed NILLA Wafers, plus more for topping

1. In a medium bowl, whip cream at high speed until soft peaks form.

2. In a large bowl, beat sweetened condensed milk, cream cheese, banana, and vanilla until smooth. Gently fold in whipped cream until well combined.

3. Fold in crushed wafers. Transfer mixture to a freezable container, allowing room for expanding. Sprinkle additional wafers on top. Freeze for 8 hours or until firm.

Raspberry Cream Cheese Puffs

Prep: 15 minutes • Cook: 20 minutes • Makes 16 puffs

There's something magical about these raspberry cream cheese puffs. The buttery, flaky dough goes amazingly with the sweetened cream cheese, fresh strawberries, and hint of almond drizzle.

1 sheet frozen puff pastry, thawed

4 ounces cream cheese, softened

¼ cup sugar

1 tablespoon milk

½ teaspoon vanilla extract

20 raspberries, divided

1 large egg, beaten

GLAZE

½ cup powdered sugar

1 tablespoon milk

¼ teaspoon almond extract

1. Preheat oven to 400 degrees F. Line a baking sheet with parchment paper. Thaw puff pastry on counter while you make filling.

2. In a medium bowl, beat cream cheese and sugar together. Add milk and vanilla. Mix until blended. Add 4 raspberries and mix until just broken up.

3. Once puff pastry is thawed enough to bend and be workable, place it on a clean surface. Cut into 16 equal squares.

4. Dollop 1 teaspoon cream cheese mixture in the center of each square. Place 1 raspberry in the center of the filling. Fold up corners, pressing them into the sauce. With a pastry brush, brush beaten egg on top of puffs.

5. Bake for 15 to 20 minutes or until puffs are golden brown. Let cool while you make glaze.

6. In a small bowl, whisk together all glaze ingredients. Add more milk if needed. Drizzle on top of puffs. Best served warm.

Cookies and Cream Brownies

Prep: 25 minutes • Cook: 35 minutes • Makes 16 bars

These brownies have a rich chocolate layer topped with a creamy cheesecake layer dotted with chunks of OREO cookies. If you're looking for a sweet treat that impresses, this is it!

CHEESECAKE LAYER

8 ounces cream cheese, softened

¼ cup sugar

1 large egg

½ teaspoon vanilla extract

BROWNIE LAYER

¾ cup unsalted butter, melted

¾ cup sugar

¾ cup brown sugar

¾ cup baking cocoa

3 large eggs, room temperature

1 teaspoon vanilla extract

¾ cup flour

1 ½ teaspoons baking powder

¼ teaspoon salt

18 OREO cookies, crushed into fine crumbs

8 OREO cookies, coarsely chopped

1. Preheat oven to 350 degrees F. Spray a 9x13-inch baking dish with nonstick cooking spray.

2. In a small bowl, beat all cheesecake layer ingredients until smooth. Set aside.

3. In a large bowl, beat butter, sugars, and cocoa until light and fluffy. Beat in eggs and vanilla. In a small bowl, whisk together flour, baking powder, and salt. Gradually stir flour mixture into cocoa mixture. Stir in crushed cookie crumbs.

4. Pour brownie mixture into prepared baking dish. Spoon cream cheese mixture over center of batter, leaving a ½-inch margin from the edge of the dish. Sprinkle coarsely chopped cookies on top.

5. Bake for 30 to 35 minutes or until a toothpick comes out with moist crumbs. Cool completely, then cut into bars. Store in refrigerator.

Caramel Apple Cookie Pizza

Prep: 20 minutes • Cook: 15 minutes • Serves 20

This caramel apple cookie pizza has a sugar cookie crust topped with cream cheese frosting. Next, we sprinkle with diced apples and pecans, then we drizzle caramel sauce on the top. It's a showstopper!

SUGAR COOKIE DOUGH

¾ cup unsalted butter, softened

¾ cup sugar

1 egg

1 teaspoon vanilla extract

2 cups flour

1 teaspoon baking powder

½ teaspoon salt

CREAM CHEESE FROSTING

4 ounces cream cheese, softened

¼ cup unsalted butter, softened

2 cups powdered sugar

½ teaspoon vanilla extract

1 to 2 tablespoons milk or heavy cream

TOPPINGS

2 cups cubed Granny Smith apple

½ cup chopped pecans

½ cup caramel sauce

1. Preheat oven to 350 degrees F. Line a 9x13-inch baking dish with parchment paper.

2. In a large bowl, beat butter and sugar until light and fluffy. Add egg and vanilla. Mix until smooth.

3. In a small bowl, whisk together flour, baking powder, and salt. Slowly add flour mixture to wet mixture until combined.

4. Press into prepared baking dish. Bake for 12 to 14 minutes or until edges just start to brown. Let cool.

5. While dough cooks, prepare cream cheese frosting. In a large bowl, beat cream cheese and butter until fluffy. Add powdered sugar, vanilla, and milk or cream. Mix slowly at first, then increase speed until light and fluffy.

6. Spread frosting on cooled crust. Sprinkle with apples and pecans. Drizzle with caramel.

SCRUMPTIOUS TIP

To help prevent your apples from browning, place your diced apples in 2 cups water with ½ teaspoon salt. Soak for 5 minutes, then rinse. This slows down the oxidizing process.

Key Lime Pie Bars

Prep: 15 minutes · Cook: 25 minutes · Serves 9

When we lived in Florida, our family's happy place was snorkeling in the Florida Keys. It was about an hour and a half from our house, and we would go there often. At every restaurant we went to, we would always order a key lime pie for dessert and make a note of our favorites. Once, we ordered as many key lime pies as we could from different restaurants in the Keys and brought them home to have a tasting contest with our friends. Our favorite pie had an almond graham cracker crust. It was tart but not too tart and was topped with fresh whipped cream. This pie was inspired by that one!

CRUST

1 cup graham cracker crumbs

1 cup sweetened toasted coconut

6 tablespoons unsalted butter, melted

¼ cup finely ground almonds

3 tablespoons sugar

¼ teaspoon ground cinnamon (optional)

FILLING

3 large egg yolks, room temperature

1 (14-ounce) can sweetened condensed milk

⅔ cup lime juice

1. Preheat oven to 350 degrees F. Line an 8x8-inch baking dish with parchment paper.

2. In a food processor, pulse crust ingredients until mixture resembles wet sand. Press mixture into an even layer in prepared pan. Bake for 8 to 10 minutes or until crust is golden brown. Cool completely.

3. Add egg yolks to the bowl of a stand mixer with the whisk attachment. Whisk eggs for 2 minutes or until yolks turn a pale yellow and thicken. Slowly whisk in sweetened condensed milk. Whisk for 2 minutes. Slowly pour in lime juice. Whisk until fully combined.

4. Pour mixture into cooled graham cracker crust. Bake for 12 to 15 minutes or until filling is set. Cool completely on a rack, then refrigerate for at least 2 hours before serving.

5. Cut into squares and serve with fresh whipped cream.

SCRUMPTIOUS TIP

Although real key limes are ideal, they are not always available. Persian limes are what most of us are familiar with, and I used them in this recipe.

Peanut Butter Chocolate Balls

Prep: 45 minutes · Makes 20 balls

My favorite food combination ever is peanut butter and chocolate. I have over a hundred peanut-butter-and-chocolate recipes on my blog. That's true love! These peanut butter balls have a silky smooth center with a crisp chocolate coating.

¾ cup creamy peanut butter (not natural)

¼ cup unsalted butter, softened

½ teaspoon vanilla extract

1 ½ cups powdered sugar

10 ounces melting chocolate

flaked sea salt (optional)

1. In a medium bowl, use a mixer to combine peanut butter, butter, and vanilla. Mix in powdered sugar a little at a time until well combined.

2. Line a baking sheet with parchment paper. Roll mixture into 1-inch balls and place on baking sheet. Place in freezer for 20 minutes.

3. After balls are done chilling, melt chocolate according to package directions. Using a fork or toothpick, dip chilled balls in chocolate coating fully. Tap fork against side to remove excess chocolate. Place on parchment paper to set. Drizzle excess chocolate on top and immediately top with sea salt if desired.

4. Store balls in refrigerator for up to 2 weeks or freeze for 2 months.

Churro Saltine Cracker Toffee

Prep: 15 minutes • Cook: 10 minutes • Makes 40 crackers

My grandma was known for her saltine cracker toffee. Because I like things with cinnamon and sugar, I came up with this white chocolate version that tastes just like a churro.

40 salted saltine crackers

1 cup unsalted butter

1 cup brown sugar

2 cups white chocolate chips

¼ cup granulated sugar

1 teaspoon ground cinnamon

1. Preheat oven to 400 degrees F. Line a baking sheet with parchment paper or foil. Place saltine crackers in a single layer on baking sheet.

2. In a small pot, bring butter and brown sugar to a boil. Boil for 3 minutes. Mixture should be a deep caramel color. Immediately pour over saltines and spread to cover crackers completely.

3. Bake crackers for 5 to 6 minutes. Mixture will get bubbly, and crackers will look like they are floating. Remove from oven and straighten any crackers that have gotten out of line.

4. Sprinkle with white chocolate chips and let sit a couple of minutes to melt. If your pan isn't hot enough, you can place it back in the oven for about a minute to get the chips to melt. Spread melted white chocolate evenly with a spatula.

5. In a small bowl, whisk together granulated sugar and cinnamon. Sprinkle evenly on top of white chocolate while it's still wet.

6. Cool completely. You can place pan in refrigerator for about 10 minutes to help white chocolate set. Once white chocolate is set, break into pieces and eat.

S'mores Brownies

Prep: 15 minutes • Cook: 50 minutes • Makes 9 brownies

These rich chocolate brownies have a graham cracker crust and are topped with pillowy marshmallows that are just starting to brown. We're bringing the campfire indoors and eating s'mores in the kitchen!

CRUST

1 ½ cups graham cracker crumbs

6 tablespoons unsalted butter, melted

1 tablespoon sugar

BROWNIES

¾ cup unsalted butter, cubed

4 ounces unsweetened baking chocolate

1 cup sugar

½ cup brown sugar

½ cup baking cocoa

3 large eggs

1 teaspoon vanilla extract

¾ cup flour

1 ½ cups mini marshmallows

1. Preheat oven to 350 degrees F. Line a 9x9-inch baking pan with parchment paper and spray with nonstick cooking spray.

2. Combine all crust ingredients in a medium bowl. Press firmly into prepared pan in an even layer. Bake for 5 to 6 minutes. Let crust cool.

3. Add butter and baking chocolate to a large microwave-safe bowl. Microwave in 30-second intervals until butter and chocolate are melted and smooth, stirring in between.

4. Stir in sugars, cocoa, eggs, and vanilla until well combined. Stir in flour until just combined. Pour onto cooled crust and bake for 30 to 35 minutes or until middle of brownies is set.

5. Sprinkle on marshmallows. Bake for about 5 minutes or until marshmallows puff up but do not turn brown.

6. Let cool completely. Cut and serve.

Blueberry Lemon Blondies

Prep: 10 minutes • Cook: 25 minutes • Makes 9 bars

These bright and cheery blueberry lemon blondies are sweet and tart. These are a fun treat to make on a summer day . . . or any day!

BLONDIES

¾ cup flour

¼ teaspoon salt

8 tablespoons unsalted butter, softened

¾ cup granulated sugar

1 teaspoon finely grated lemon zest

2 large eggs

1 tablespoon fresh lemon juice

¾ cup blueberries

LEMON GLAZE

½ cup powdered sugar

1 tablespoon fresh lemon juice

1 teaspoon finely grated lemon zest

1. Preheat oven to 350 degrees F. Spray an 8-inch square pan with nonstick cooking spray.

2. In medium bowl, whisk together flour and salt. Set aside.

3. In the large bowl of a stand mixer, beat butter, sugar, and lemon zest on medium speed until light and fluffy, about 3 minutes, scraping down the sides as needed.

4. Add eggs one at a time, beating well after each addition, about 20 seconds each. Add lemon juice and mix to combine.

5. Reduce speed to low and add flour mixture, mixing until just combined. Fold in blueberries.

6. Spoon batter into prepared pan. Bake for 20 to 25 minutes or until toothpick comes out clean. Cool completely.

7. While blondies cook, prepare lemon glaze. Whisk together all lemon glaze ingredients.

8. Drizzle glaze over brownies and let sit until hardened. Cut into slices and serve.

Sheet Pan Pecan Pie

Prep: 15 minutes • Cook: 50 minutes • Makes 28 squares

You will never make regular pecan pie again after making this sheet pan version. Layers of toasted pecans, a gooey filling, and a flaky pastry crust make this divine.

---

2 refrigerated pie crusts, room temperature

6 large eggs

1 cup light corn syrup

1 cup brown sugar

½ cup unsalted butter, melted

1 tablespoon vanilla extract

4 cups pecan halves

1. Preheat oven to 350 degrees F. Line a 12x17-inch baking sheet with parchment paper.

2. Overlap pie crust edges and roll into an approximately 13x18-inch rectangle (slightly bigger than baking sheet so the crust reaches up the sides of the pan). Place pie crust on prepared baking sheet and crimp pie edges. Place in freezer while preparing filling.

3. In a large bowl, whisk together eggs, corn syrup, brown sugar, melted butter, and vanilla. Stir in pecans.

4. Take crust out of freezer and pour filling into crust.

5. Carefully transfer to oven. Bake for 45 to 50 minutes or until center is set and crust is golden.

6. Cool completely and cut into squares.

Brownie Cookies

Prep: 15 minutes · Cook: 15 minutes · Makes 12 cookies

These brownie cookies have a crisp edge with a chewy, fudgy center. They are the best of both the brownie and cookie worlds.

⅔ cup flour

2 tablespoons unsweetened cocoa powder

1 teaspoon baking powder

¼ teaspoon salt

8 ounces semisweet baking chocolate, chopped

¼ cup unsalted butter, cubed

2 large eggs, room temperature

½ cup sugar

½ cup brown sugar

1 teaspoon vanilla extract

½ cup semisweet chocolate chips

flaked salt for topping

1. Preheat oven to 350 degrees F. Line 2 baking sheets with parchment paper.

2. In a medium bowl, whisk together flour, cocoa, baking powder, and salt.

3. Place chopped baking chocolate and butter in a microwave-safe bowl. Heat in microwave in 30-second intervals until melted, stirring in between. Let mixture cool slightly.

4. With a stand or hand mixer, beat eggs, sugars, and vanilla in a large bowl for 5 minutes on medium speed.

5. Slowly pour in melted chocolate mixture and mix until combined. Add flour mixture and mix until just combined. Fold in chocolate chips. Batter will be wet like brownie batter.

6. Using a cookie scoop, place heaping tablespoons of dough 3 inches apart on prepared pans. Cookies will spread.

7. Bake for 12 to 14 minutes or until tops are set. Immediately sprinkle with flaked salt. Let cookies cool on pan. Keep stored in an airtight container for up to 2 days.

index

References to photographs are in **bold**.

about the author

CHRISTY DENNEY is the author of the popular food blog "The Girl Who Ate Everything," which is filled with a wide-variety of tried-and-true recipes. Her test kitchen now includes her five children and her husband, who played thirteen years in the NFL with the Miami Dolphins. Christy worked for General Mills as a writer and recipe developer as well as seven years in the Betty Crocker Food-Styling Kitchens. In addition, she played the viola for ten years so music is a big part of her life. Thus, she can usually be found in the kitchen with the tunes cranking.